I0884136

CLEAR AND PRESENT DANGER

SCHENCK V. UNITED STATES

WE SUPPOR
THE FIRST
AMENDME

FIRST AMENDMENT CASES

CLEAR AND PRESENT DANGER

SCHENCK V. UNITED STATES

By Susan Dudley Gold

Cavendish Square
New York

With special thanks to David M. O'Brien, Spicer Professor, Department of Politics, University of Virginia, for his expert review of this manuscript.

First Edition

Website: cavendishsq.com

CPSIA Compliance Information:
Batch #WW14CSQ

All websites were available and accurate when this book was sent to press.

LIBRARY OF CONGRESS CATALOGING-IN-PUBLICATION DATA
Gold, Susan Dudley, author. Clear and present danger : Schenck v. United States / Susan Dudley Gold. pages cm — (First Amendment cases)
Includes bibliographical references and index
ISBN 978-1-62712-387-7 (hardcover)
ISBN 978-1-62712-389-1 (paperback)
ISBN 978-1-62712-388-4 (ebook)
1. Freedom of speech—United States—Juvenile literature. 2. Trials (Sedition)—United States—Juvenile literature. 3. Schenck, Charles—Trials, litigation, etc.—Juvenile literature. I. Title. KF4772.G65 2014 342.7308'53—dc23
2013033262

Series Designer: Michael Nelson
Art Director: Anahid Hamparian
Photo Research: Custom Communications, Inc.

The photographs in this book are used by permission and through the courtesy of: Associated Press: Kin Cheung, cover; AP, 2 (*bottom*); Moscow Pullman Daily News, 115; Stefan Wermuth, 121. Library of Congress: 8, 96; Willard and Dorothy Straight Collection, 26; George Grantham Bain, 34, 47, 49; Harris & Ewing Collection, 39, 71 (*left*); W. F. Powers Co. Litho., 51; Eagle Lithographing Co., 55; National Photo Co. Collection, 71 (*right*); WPA Poster Collection, 107. Granger Collection NYC: 15, 90, 92. Bridgeman Art Library: Look and Learn, 23. Getty: Universal Images Group, 24; Time & Life Pictures, 64. Corbis: Bettmann, 41; 76; Collection of the Supreme Court of the United States: Barnett Clinedinst Jr., 60.

Printed in the United States of America

CONTENTS

FIRST AMENDMENT

THE FIRST AMENDMENT

Congress shall make no law respecting an establishment of religion, or prohibiting the free exercise thereof; or abridging the freedom of speech, or of the press; or the right of the people peaceably to assemble, and to petition the Government for a redress of grievances.

—*U.S. Constitution, Amendment I*

INTRODUCTION

"A Clear and Present Danger"

IN ITS FIRST IMPORTANT DECISION ON FREE speech, a unanimous U.S. Supreme Court ruled on March 3, 1919, that the government can punish "dangerous" speech only if it meets certain requirements. The decision, in *Schenck v. United States*, established a standard, called the "clear and present danger" test, to determine whether or not speech is so inflammatory that it no longer qualifies for First Amendment protections.

The ruling upheld the convictions of Socialists Elizabeth Baer and Charles Schenck, who were found guilty of violating the Espionage Act of 1917 because of their link to flyers urging opposition to the draft during World War I. Both served short prison sentences as a result.

The defendants in *Schenck* argued that the act violated their constitutional right to free speech. The flyers urged young men not to register for the draft and encouraged people to sign petitions against it. The Espionage Act of 1917, which Congress passed at the outset of World War I, not only made such actions illegal, but also banned words that encouraged the illegal behavior.

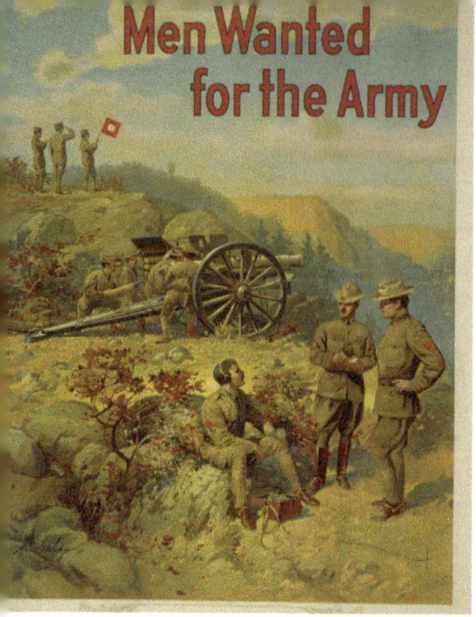

Recruitment poster designed to encourage young men to join the army during World War I.

The Supreme Court found that national security, especially in times of war, overrode unrestricted free speech. Justice Oliver Wendell Holmes Jr. delivered the Court's decision. He noted that the outcome of every case depended on the circumstances surrounding it. Words that might be acceptable—or at least tolerated—during peacetime might present such "a clear and present danger" to the nation at war that they would no longer be protected under the First Amendment. In *Schenck v. United States*, the Court ruled that Congress had a right to ban the antidraft pamphlets because they threatened the nation's ability to recruit soldiers and thus to wage war against Germany.

Holmes's "clear and present danger" rule rested on an old English method of judging whether speech should be suppressed, called the "bad tendency" test. If the words showed that the speaker intended to harm the nation (had a "bad tendency"), then the government was justified in suppressing such speech. Just months after formulating his test, however, Holmes called for a more moderate approach to provide broader protections for speech. In his dissent in *Abrams v. United States*, Holmes modified his test to apply only when the danger is "imminent" and the intent is to do immediate harm. It took many years, however, before the Court adopted Holmes's revision.

The Supreme Court justices who ruled in the *Schenck* case faced an age-old dilemma: How does a democracy balance safety against freedom? In other words, how much freedom do citizens have to sacrifice to protect the nation? Or, considered another way, how much insecurity can citizens tolerate to retain their freedoms?

These are simple questions with complex answers. For example, parents might believe they are keeping their children safe by never allowing them to go near the water. But what happens when they take a boat ride as adults and the vessel sinks? Because their parents kept them away from the water as children, they never learned to swim. As a result, they lack the very tools they need to save themselves.

In a democracy, citizens use information gleaned from all types of sources to make decisions—and cast their votes—on political candidates and issues that range from the local dog ordinance to amendments to the U.S. Constitution. These sources include radical and conventional newspapers, speeches and informal dialogue, comedy routines and parodies, televised interviews and debates, blogs and websites, and pamphlets, brochures, and leaflets. These are the tools through which citizens express their opinions and learn the views of others.

The First Amendment protects the right of all Americans to express their views freely. It guarantees the freedom of the press to publish without oversight by the government. What happens, though, if some of the views are threatening? Do citizens still have the right to voice such views? Can the government stop the press from publishing tracts that urge people to break the law? How much danger do such expressions pose?

In *Schenck v. United States*, the Supreme Court of 1919 opened the door to exceptions to First Amendment protection of free speech, especially during wartime. The ruling has been cited in dozens of cases at the Supreme Court level and many more times by lower courts. Through the years, the Court has interpreted the test in different ways, putting some categories of speech under the protection of the First Amendment and eliminating that protection from other types of speech.

The Court has never overturned the *Schenck* ruling, and although Congress repealed the amendments to the Espionage Act known as the Sedition Act, parts of the original law remain on the books today. There are still situations in which the Court has allowed limits on speech, most related to national security. But even Holmes himself, in his dissent in *Abrams*, expressed reservations about punishing dangerous speech too broadly. He said: "Congress certainly cannot forbid all effort to change the mind of the country."

CHAPTER ONE

"WAKE UP, AMERICA!"

ON AUGUST 13, 1917, THE EXECUTIVE COMMITtee of the Philadelphia branch of the Socialist Party voted to print fifteen thousand leaflets and distribute them to the young men in the area who had been drafted to serve in U.S. military operations during World War I. The antiwar pamphlets urged the men to write to their congressmen and come to Socialist headquarters to sign a petition supporting the repeal of the law requiring the draft.

Socialists promote a classless society in which workers share in the fruits of their labor. Most U.S. Socialists believe this can be accomplished through economic reforms without an overthrow of the government.

Elizabeth Baer, a member of the Socialist Party executive committee, recorded the minutes of the meeting, and Charles Schenck, general secretary of the group, took on the task of having the pamphlets printed. On August 20 the executive committee met again to address envelopes in which the newly printed flyers would be mailed. The members voted to give Schenck $125 to cover postage for the mailings.

Emblazoned across one side of the leaflet was the heading: "Long Live the Constitution of the United States! Wake up, America! Your Liberties Are in Danger!" Below the headline, the flyer carried Section 1 of the Thirteenth Amendment, which prohibits slavery and involuntary servitude. The leaflet outlined the Socialist Party's premise that the draft was a form of involuntary servitude and therefore violated the Thirteenth Amendment. "A conscript [soldier who is drafted into military service] is little better than a convict," the tract asserted. "When you conscript a man and compel him to go abroad to fight against his will, you violate the most sacred right of personal liberty."

The flyer appealed to citizens to write to Congress saying the draft law should be repealed. "Do not submit to intimidation," the flyer said. It encouraged readers to come to Socialist headquarters to sign a petition for its repeal. "Help us wipe out this stain upon the Constitution!" the pamphlet proclaimed. "Long live the Republic!" At the end of the appeal was a notice that the Socialist Party Book Store had books on Socialism for sale.

The other side of the flyer, headlined "Assert Your

Rights!," contained more of the same. Under the title, the circular carried sections of the Constitution, including the First Amendment's freedom of religion clause. It exhorted all men who were subject to the draft to stand up for their rights and assert their opposition to the law. "In lending tacit or silent consent to the conscription law, in neglecting to assert your rights, you are (whether unknowingly or not) helping to condone and support a most infamous and insidious conspiracy to abridge and destroy the sacred and cherished rights of a free people." The flyer continued, "The people of this country did not vote in favor of war. At the last election they voted against war." After expressing opposition to U.S. participation in a war overseas, the flyer ended with two questions: "In this world crisis where do you stand? Are you with the forces of liberty and light or war and darkness?"

Schenck took the flyers to the local post office and mailed them. Shortly afterward, government officials came to the Socialists' headquarters. The officers found Schenck in the office, arrested him and several of his associates, and confiscated the minutes of the party's meetings as well as three bundles of antiwar pamphlets. The officials also took with them a number of newspaper clippings listing names of men who had been drafted.

An indictment filed in U.S. District Court in Pennsylvania on September 15, 1917, charged Schenck, Baer, Charles Sehl, Jacob H. Root, and William J. Higgins with conspiring to obstruct the draft. The Socialists were indicted on three charges:

- Conspiracy to print and circulate materials to men drafted into the military in order to "cause insubordination, disloyalty, mutiny and refusal of duty in the military and naval forces of the United States and to obstruct the recruiting and enlistment" of the men, an Espionage Act violation;
- Conspiracy to use the U.S. postal service to deliver materials banned by the Espionage Act;
- Knowingly using the U.S. postal service to illegally deliver banned materials.

The trial opened on December 17, 1917, in federal district court in Philadelphia. Henry John Nelson, a radical Philadelphia attorney who had served as noted anarchist Emma Goldman's lawyer, represented the Socialists. Nelson maintained that the pamphlet circulated by his clients simply aimed to express the view that the draft was unconstitutional and advocated for its repeal. The district attorney's office argued that the defendants went beyond merely expressing an opinion. Their actions, the prosecuting attorneys said, violated the Espionage Act because the pamphlet tried to persuade draft-age men to break the law and evade military service.

The prosecutor produced the minutes of the meet-

American Socialist poster produced in 1911 criticizing capitalism.

ings of the local Socialist Party's executive committee, which outlined the plan to distribute the pamphlets. Baer told the court she had written the minutes, which were found in Schenck's office at party headquarters. During testimony, Schenck acknowledged he served as the paid general secretary of the Philadelphia Socialist group. Witnesses testified that Schenck ordered the flyers to be printed and directed their distribution. Consequently, the pamphlets were mailed to about fifteen thousand young men in the area who had been drafted. Later testimony showed that many of the pamphlets were never delivered.

On the third day of the trial, Samuel O. Wynne, a postal inspector, testified that several people had filed complaints with the post office that they had received the antiwar flyer and an accompanying letter from the Socialist Party. He said he had also been contacted by postal supervisors at various post offices throughout Philadelphia about the pamphlets. Wynne testified that he ordered the supervisors to hold any further envelopes containing the pamphlets and send them to his office. He received about six hundred envelopes containing the Socialist material from the post offices. Wynne said postal officials identified the unopened envelopes as those containing the antiwar material because they were mailed at the same time from the same place as the ones that brought about complaints, and they had identical handwriting on the front. In some cases, the envelopes were thin enough to see the pamphlet inside. Wynne said he had no way of knowing who mailed the envelopes, since none contained return addresses. He also acknowledged that some of the blocked mail might have contained private correspondence.

Wynne testified that he notified the U.S. Attorney's office, which obtained a search warrant and a warrant for Schenck's arrest. Wynne accompanied agents on the search of Socialist Party headquarters.

Later in the day Louis M. Passavello, a young man who had registered for the draft as required by law, testified that he had received the Socialists' pamphlet in the mail in August 1917. After reading it, he said he reported it to postal inspectors because he "didn't think such literature should be sent through the mail." Passavello said that reading the circular did not cause him "to act in an insubordinate way" toward the government or try to evade the draft. In fact, he said, it made him even more vigilant in fulfilling his patriotic duties.

Another young man, Horace F. Banks, testified next. Banks, who had been drafted and was based at Camp Meade in Maryland, identified an envelope with his name and address on it. The mail had never been delivered to him. Inside was the circular from the Socialist Party. The envelope was postmarked August 28, 1917, from Passyunk Station in Philadelphia. Several other young men, whose names had been reported in the newspapers as having registered for the draft, gave similar testimony. They told attorney Nelson that the pamphlet would not have caused them to become disloyal to the nation. The prosecution never produced even one drafted man who said he resisted serving in the military because of the message conveyed in the Socialists' flyer.

At the end of the trial, District Judge J. Whitaker Thompson questioned the prosecutor's case against Sehl, Root, and Higgins. "In a criminal case of conspiracy, you have got to prove the people who are charged with being conspirators took some part in the conspiracy," he said.

"There is no evidence at all . . . to show they took any part in the sending out of these circulars." As a result, the district attorney withdrew the charges against the three men. Judge Thompson let stand the charges against Schenck and Baer, however, ruling that "there is sufficient evidence to make out a. . . . case [against the two]."

Nelson asked the judge to instruct the jury that citizens should be charged only for illegal actions, not words. "Under the First Amendment to the Constitution, freedom of speech and of the press cannot be abridged, and people can only be held responsible for the results of their utterance," he said. "If, therefore, the government has not shown you that any injury was caused to the [military] service of the United States or to the United States as a result of the utterances alleged against these defendants, then your verdict should be 'not guilty,'" Nelson said.

Judge Thompson, however, took issue with that statement. He noted that it did not matter in a conspiracy case if the aim of the defendants had not been met. If the evidence showed beyond a reasonable doubt that the defendants had conspired to commit an illegal act and if an illegal act had indeed been done, then the jury should find them guilty, Thompson said. It was not up to the judge or the jury to determine whether the draft law was constitutional, he said. Thompson reminded the jury that all citizens had a "right to speak and write and urge other people to speak and write in order to obtain the repeal of any law which does not appeal to them." But, he noted, while citizens had the right to persuade people to work for the repeal of a law, they did not, under the Espionage Act, have a right to incite others to break that law.

Schenck and Baer were found guilty as charged, but the jury recommended that the court be merciful in sentencing them. The two defendants asked for a new trial, claiming that there was insufficient evidence to convict them. They contended that the court should not have relied on the minutes to show a conspiracy. Judge Thompson denied the request on March 1, 1918. The records were "clearly admissible" against the two defendants and showed "a common design" to carry out the plot, the judge said.

On March 21, 1918, Judge Thompson sentenced Schenck to six months in prison at the Mercer County Jail in Trenton, New Jersey, and ordered him to pay the costs of the trial. Baer, a medical doctor, was sentenced to ninety days in jail, to be served in the Philadelphia County Prison, and ordered to pay a $500 fine and court costs. Under the Espionage Act, they could have been given twenty-year prison sentences and fines of up to $10,000 on the two counts for which they were convicted.

That same day, Schenck and Baer appealed the decision to the U.S. Supreme Court. They claimed that the district court had committed errors in the way the trial was conducted. During the appeal period, the defendants remained free on a bond of $5,000. The case, backed by the National Civil Liberties Bureau (NCLB), would be a test case to challenge the constitutionality of the Espionage Act. The NCLB, which focused on protecting the rights of conscientious objectors during the war, changed its name to the American Civil Liberties Union in 1920 and broadened its scope to work for civil rights for all Americans.

WAR AND PEACE

At the time of the incident and the trial, the United States was embroiled in the Great War, the first global war, later known as World War I. Hostilities began in the summer of 1914, but the United States did not enter the war until April 6, 1917. For some Americans, family heritage determined their stance on the war in Europe, which initially pitted Germany and Austria against France and Great Britain. Thus some German Americans supported Germany in the conflict, while those of English and French descent positioned themselves on the side of their European relatives. Most citizens wanted America to stay out of the war. A survey of U.S. newspaper editors in 1914 revealed that a large majority (almost 66 percent) did not express support for either side in the conflict.

When the war began in Europe, President Woodrow Wilson and most of America's leaders favored neutrality. In a message to Congress on August 18, 1914, the president told his fellow citizens, "Every man who really loves America will act and speak in the true spirit of neutrality." He urged Americans to stay loyal to the United States, not to divide over support for the various European combatants. "The United States must be neutral in fact, as well as in name, during these days that are to try men's souls," Wilson said in a reference to an oft-quoted phrase by founding father Thomas Paine.

President Wilson ran for reelection in 1916 on a platform promising that the United States would not enter what many Americans considered to be Europe's war. Campaigning under the slogan "He kept us out of war," Wilson won the election, but less than three months after beginning his second term of office, on April 2, 1917, the president asked Congress to declare war on Germany to make the world "safe for democracy." In the months before the declaration, German submarines began an all-out attack on merchant vessels as well as military ships in the Atlantic. These attacks, which sank several American ships and killed U.S. citizens aboard vessels of other nations, helped convince U.S. leaders that war was inevitable. By 1917 American businesses had a vested interest in a British victory. U.S. bankers had approved more than $2.1 billion in loans to Great Britain and its allies, and American shippers had lucrative contracts supplying the allied countries with supplies and munitions.

During the years leading up to World War I, the peace movement in the United States blossomed, attracting many prominent Americans. President Wilson himself had at one time been a member of the American Peace Society. Auto tycoon Henry Ford and other U.S. business leaders sailed to Europe in an effort to negotiate a settlement to end the war there in late 1915 and 1916. Industrial giant Andrew Carnegie set up the Carnegie Endowment for International Peace and pushed for the establishment of a league of nations to resolve differences.

War fever had been mounting, however, since the sinking of the British ocean liner *Lusitania* by a German U-boat on May 7, 1915, off the coast of Ireland. The ship sailed from New York on May 1 with munitions, food, and other supplies for Great Britain and its allies. Among those lost in the tragedy were 123 Americans. The U.S. military would later use the slogan "Remember the *Lusitania*!" on posters encouraging men to enlist.

All but six senators and fifty House members voted for the declaration of war against Germany in early April 1917. Congress issued a formal declaration on April 6 authorizing President Wilson to direct the nation's military forces to wage war on Germany. Six weeks later, on May 18, 1917, the Selective Draft Law went into effect. The law required all U.S. males between twenty-one and thirty to register for the draft. This was later expanded to include men between the ages of eighteen and forty-five.

The sinking of the *Lusitania* off the coast of Ireland in 1915.

Exemptions were provided for disabled men, certain state and federal officials and those holding essential jobs, religious leaders and members of three sects (Quakers, Amish, and Church of the Brethren) who objected to war for religious reasons, men already in the military, and those who were the sole support of their families.

Congress passed the bill at Wilson's request to have enough soldiers for the war effort. In anticipation of the bill, the War Department had already set up a nationwide system to register and draft American men who met the law's requirements. Twenty-four million men filled out draft registration cards, and 2.8 million were called up to serve in the armed forces during World War I. Names were drawn from a giant lottery of draft-eligible men.

Once the United States entered the war, the public

On April 2, 1917, President Woodrow Wilson asked Congress to declare war against Germany. Four days later Congress issued a formal declaration of war.

attitude began to shift toward supporting the nation's military actions. Many Americans, however, continued to oppose U.S. involvement in the war. Socialists, pacifist groups, trade unions, and others, including such prominent citizens as Helen Keller, the social activist who was blind and deaf, and sociologist Jane Addams, participated in the antiwar campaign. The largest organized group to oppose U.S. intervention in the war was the Socialist Party of America, which had nearly 120,000 members at its peak in 1912.

That year the party's candidate for president, Eugene V. Debs, won more than 900,000 votes, 6 percent of those cast, the largest vote for a Socialist candidate ever recorded in the United States. Another indication of the party's support among Americans was the popularity of its journal, *Appeal to Reason*. The publication, whose contributors included novelist Jack London and Pulitzer Prize–winning author Upton Sinclair, sold 760,000 copies a week in 1913.

The Socialists made repeal of the draft one of their major efforts in 1917. Thousands of people gathered to protest the draft at rallies held throughout the country. At a rally held at the end of May that filled Madison Square Garden in New York City, one speaker warned against using unconstitutional measures to wage war. He included the draft in those measures. It would be a tragedy, he said, if America, in its efforts to make the world "safe for democracy," destroyed its own democracy.

Participants at the rally adopted a resolution urging Congress to allow exemptions for all conscientious objectors, not just those who belonged to certain religious sects. The resolution also criticized the draft law as unconstitutional and a violation of the Thirteenth Amendment's ban on involuntary servitude.

GOVERNMENT PROPAGANDA

To silence critics and win the support of the American public, the federal government established the Committee on Public Information (CPI), headed by George Creel, to promote the war effort. It was the first

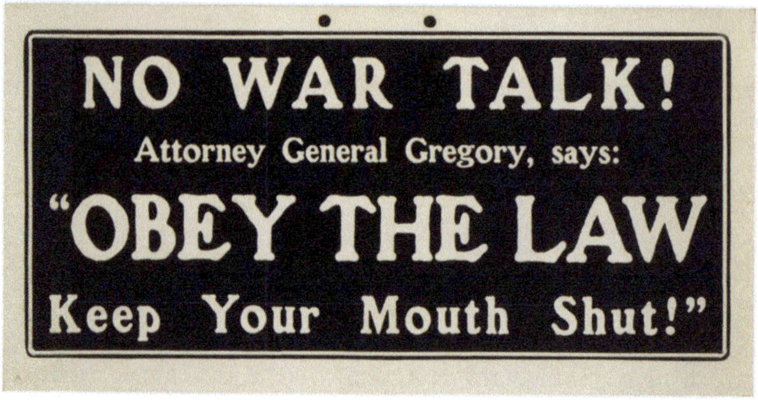

Posters warned Americans not to talk about World War I.

official propaganda campaign directed by the government toward American citizens. Created a week after the declaration of war, the CPI ran a massive advertising campaign focused on "the written word, the spoken word, and…motion picture[s]." The drive targeted almost every form of media: newspapers, magazines, films, pamphlets, library resources, books, and educational materials.

Celebrities recruited by the committee spoke at sites across the nation on the need to support American soldiers and the cause for which they fought. Local volunteers delivered talks at county fairs, churches, town halls, and even at movie theaters during the four-minute break it took to switch movie reels. These so-called Four Minute Men gave more than 755,000 speeches over the course of the war, addressing millions of Americans.

During the talks, speakers followed the government line on the war. Although they used their own words, these volunteer orators consulted bulletins provided periodically by CPI for facts, topics, and "talking points." The bulletins, all part of the nationally run propaganda campaign, painted pacifists as traitors, glorified young men who enlisted, and criticized mothers who did not want their sons to join the military. Women volunteers also participated by talking to women's groups and speaking at children's matinees. Schools became involved in the effort by holding speaking competitions for students on patriotic topics.

The *Ladies' Home Journal*, one of the day's leading women's magazines, at the CPI's request, printed pro-war posters and wrote editorials praising the government's war efforts. Illustrators contributed pro-war drawings for government pamphlets and magazine covers.

The CPI worked with newspapers, providing news items and releases focused on generating support for the war. Magazines and newspapers provided free space for public service announcements from CPI. The committee also printed its own daily newspaper and provided items to foreign-language papers in the United States. The CPI even had a bureau of cartoons, which influenced the content of comics appearing in newspapers.

Another division of the organization published hundreds of books, pamphlets, and bulletins promoting the war and America's part in it. Practically every segment of the U.S. population received attention. The government agency distributed pamphlets aimed at teachers, schoolchildren, women, African Americans, union members, immigrants, and many others.

Librarians across the country screened books in their collections and removed those that criticized war. A library director in Iowa reported burning pro-German books donated to the library. Many librarians believed it was their patriotic duty to protect patrons from books that were radical, pacifist, or supported Germany.

The film industry provided another venue for government propaganda. The CPI produced a weekly newsreel, a short film containing the official government report on the war. These were shown at movie theaters before the main show. Several movie stars, including Charlie Chaplin, Mary Pickford, and Douglas Fairbanks, helped sell war bonds to fund U.S. military operations. In addition, Hollywood produced a number of box-office hits with war-related themes, which portrayed the U.S. war effort in a positive light. Among the most popular was *Shoulder Arms*, a comedy in which Chaplin starred as a hapless French soldier. These were silent films; full-length feature films with sound did not appear until the late 1920s.

The CPI's propaganda campaign not only won the public's support for the war effort but also created an atmosphere in which dissent was not tolerated. Groups like the Socialists that did not support America's entry into the war faced overwhelming opposition from a public sold on the war's righteousness.

CHAPTER TWO

ESPIONAGE ACT OF 1917

TWO MONTHS AFTER VOTING TO DECLARE war, Congress passed the Espionage Act. This put the force of law into the effort to quell dissent. Even before war broke out, Congress began debating an espionage bill designed to protect defense secrets. The Wilson administration pressured legislators to pass the bill, which was recommended by the attorney general as well as the secretaries of state, war, and the navy.

The initial bill gave the president sweeping powers to act against foreign agents and authority to enforce a complete ban on information relating to the nation's armed forces, as well as any criticism of the government and the military. The ban included reports in newspapers and other media. Drastic penalties were proposed for those who provided information to the enemy or even to those who possessed such information without permission.

President Woodrow Wilson justified the need for the Espionage Act by insisting that the nation needed to be protected from the few "who cannot be relied upon and whose interests or desires will lead to actions on their part highly dangerous to the Nation in the midst of a war."

Once before, Congress had enacted a law designed to curb printed materials critical of the government. In 1798 Federalists in Congress passed a sweeping law to muzzle Republican critics, among them Thomas Jefferson. The Sedition Act of 1798 made it illegal for anyone to publish "any false, scandalous and malicious writings" against the government of the United States, Congress, or the president. Those who violated the law faced a fine and a jail sentence.

The Federalists argued that the law was needed because of attacks on U.S. merchant ships by mercenaries supported by the French Revolutionary government. The so-called Undeclared Naval War with France raged from 1798 to 1800. The Sedition Act did not expire until 1801, when Jefferson became president.

In February 1917 Senator Lee S. Overman, chair of the judiciary subcommittee reviewing the espionage bill, argued that the dangers of the world situation demanded such safeguards to protect the nation's security. Overman, a North Carolina Democrat, said he had been told that there were 100,000 spies in the United States. He said the figure came from "creditable reports from Secret Service men." The claim, never substantiated, nevertheless spread fear of enemy agents among the public.

The Senate Judiciary Committee issued a favorable report on the bill after reviewing it behind closed doors. A small group of opponents led by Senator Albert B. Cummins, a Republican from Iowa, called the bill "a menace to the liberties of the people" that would allow the president to set up a military dictatorship. "We have gone mad," Cummins told his fellow senators. "We have forgotten that we live in a republic. We're thinking only of spies—of German spies, of English spies. . . . There may be times when the business of the government should be kept secret in times of war, but at other times it is unjust and un-American."

Before final action could be taken on the bill, the United States declared war against Germany. Even so, by mid-April a coalition of Republicans and Democrats had lined up against this attempt to silence the press. "I would put no restriction on the American press that is not absolutely necessary to the salvation of the Republic," said Senator Charles S. Thomas, a Colorado Democrat, during discussion of the bill. "Once the right of the press is invaded, the rights of the people will be. I would rather see no law at all; I would rather take my chances under existing laws than to see a statute like this passed by the Congress of the United States." Several other senators expressed similar objections. Senator William E. Borah, a Republican from Idaho, described the effort to censor the press as a flagrant violation of the Constitution. Massachusetts Republican senator Henry Cabot Lodge agreed. "I think to attempt to deny to the press all legitimate criticism either of Congress or the Executive is going very dangerously far."

The American Union Against Militarism and other peace groups bitterly opposed the bill. Members noted that pacifists who opposed war, newspapers that criticized the military, and whistle-blowers who exposed wrongdoing and corruption in army contracts could face prison sentences of thirty years to life and fines of up to $10,000 for violating the bill's provisions.

Under the bill, violators were defined as "whoever in time of war shall by any means spread or make reports or statements or convey information with intent to cause dissatisfaction in or interfere with the operations or success of the military or naval forces of the United States." Another section of the bill banned anyone not authorized to do so from collecting, recording, publishing, communicating, or attempting to elicit any information on military operations, the armed forces, or "relating to the public defense" which might be "useful to the enemy."

At hearings of the House Judiciary Committee, several groups testified against the bill and called for changes. Gilbert E. Roe, a lawyer from New York, said that there might be good reason for dissatisfaction in war-related or government operations. "If there should arise well-founded reason for disaffection, do you want to put on the statute books a law that would prevent any one from pointing out the evils and correcting them?" he asked committee members. Union official Arthur E. Holder argued that workers should be able to report corruption at war plants for the good of the country. "If we know that things are not done on the square, if we know that grafters are taking advantage of the patriotic sentiment of the people and squeezing war profits, . . . we will make our protest whatever be the outcome," he said.

Social activist Jane Addams, the first American woman to win the Nobel Peace Prize, expressed concern that the bill as written would penalize pacifist groups for speaking their views and working with international organizations for world peace. In answer to a question by the committee, Addams said she did not know whether she would speak out against the draft once it was authorized by Congress. "I am constantly agitating against laws that are in existence," she said. "I do not know what discussion would arise over the compulsory service issue." The *Schenck* case would revolve around that very issue.

After secret consideration of the bill, the Senate Judiciary Committee gave it a favorable report and sent it to the full Senate for debate on April 14. The

Members of the Women's Peace Party, including Jane Addams, traveled aboard the *Noordam* to The Hague to participate in the first International Congress of Women. Many of the women also participated in Henry Ford's peace mission in 1915.

action brought renewed objections to the bill. The press mounted a national campaign against provisions that interfered with newspapers' ability to ask questions of and report on the government. Former newspaper editor J. Hampton Moore, who served as U.S. representative to Pennsylvania, called the press restrictions "drastic" and said the provisions "would cause trouble to innocent parties." Carter Glass, publisher of the *Lynchburg News* in Virginia and also a member of Congress, said it was "nonsense to enact legislation which, on its face, would make a newspaper man guilty were he to ask a simple question concerning military affairs."

"The freedom of the press may be extinguished," the *New York Times* warned in an editorial on the bill. "It [the bill] would take away the right of the people to know what the Government is doing, and how it is doing it, and it would deprive the Government of the invaluable aid of enlightened public opinion and of the guidance of the public's not less enlightened criticism." Newspapers in Missouri, Louisiana, Nebraska, Massachusetts, California, Pennsylvania, Rhode Island, Tennessee, and Washington, D.C., all called on Congress to revise the bill. "Were it possible to suppress legitimate newspaper criticism in time of war, every incompetent official, every dishonest business would be the gainer, while the whole country would suffer," wrote the *Kansas City Star* in Missouri.

Under such pressure, both houses revised the censorship portion of the bill. The revisions, however, did not appease the press or its supporters. After delaying a vote on the matter for several days, opponents won a victory in the House on May 4 when members voted 220 to 167 to throw out the entire section censoring the press.

The victory turned to defeat later in the day, when the House voted 190 to 185 for a substitute provision that left the censorship rules intact. The substitute version, unlike the original provision, stipulated that violators could have a jury trial and that the jury would decide whether published information could be useful to the enemy. Many of the censorship opponents had left the House after the first vote, thinking that no further action would be taken on the bill that evening. The final bill won House approval on a vote of 260 to 105.

The press and other advocates of free speech shifted their efforts to the Senate, where debate continued on the bill. Senators proposed various amendments to modify the censorship provision. Senator William Fosgate Kirby, an Arkansas Democrat, attempted to make the bill even more drastic with a proposal to set up a censorship board, which would have had the power to suspend publication of newspapers that printed unauthorized information. Senators apparently viewed the suggestion as preposterous, because they laughed openly at the idea. One senator "shook with amusement" after Kirby presented his proposal.

On May 12 the Senate, in a razor-thin 39-to-38 vote, eliminated the censorship provision from the espionage bill. Sixteen Democrats and twenty-three Republicans made up the majority. The vote repudiated President Wilson's efforts and heavy lobbying for the provision, which would have given him power to punish reporters and newspapers for publishing articles critical of the government and the armed forces.

Since the House and the Senate versions of the bill differed, delegates from both bodies met to hammer out a single statute. The delegates formed a conference committee to work out the differences in the two bills. Once the conference delegates agreed on a compromise bill, it would be taken back to the House and the Senate for final votes. If both houses approved the revised bill, it would be sent to the president for his signature.

President Wilson continued to insist that press censorship was "absolutely necessary" to protect the public safety. He met with the three senators on the conference committee to urge them to pass a bill with censorship provisions without delay, but Senator Overman said it was "extremely doubtful" that the Senate would approve any such measure. Nevertheless, the conference hammered out an agreement that included a modified section that allowed the president to determine what war-related news the newspapers could print.

Under heavy pressure from newspapers and Republican members of Congress who opposed press restrictions, the House repudiated the milder version in a 184–144 vote on May 31 and eliminated the censorship provision altogether. Representative George S. Graham, a Republican from Pennsylvania, led the opposition to the provision, which he called a "pernicious section." Thirty-six Democrats joined Republicans in the final vote to do away with the press gag. Administration supporters promoted censorship as a patriotic necessity, but opponents argued that American troops would be better served if newspapers were allowed to report improper conditions that endangered soldiers' lives. "How can you criticize when criticism is needed without being able to state the basis of your criticism?" asked Graham.

The Senate agreed to the House revision, and the bill went to President Wilson. After the president signed the bill into law, on June 16, 1917, the Department of Justice issued a news release calling the act "one of the most important pieces of legislation enacted since the declaration of the state of war."

ESPIONAGE ACT OF 1917, SECTION 3

> Whoever, when the United States is at war, shall willfully make or convey false reports or false statements with intent to interfere with the operation or success of the military or naval forces of the United States . . . and whoever, when the United States is at war, shall willfully cause or attempt to cause insubordination, disloyalty, mutiny, or refusal of duty, in the military or naval forces of the United States, or shall willfully obstruct the recruiting or enlistment service of the United States . . . shall be punished by a fine of not more than $10,000 or imprisonment for not more than twenty years, or both.

Although Congress stripped the bill of a press censorship provision, the statute retained its ban on other material critical of the nation's war effort. Among its provisions, the Espionage Act gave Postmaster General Albert Sidney Burleson almost complete power to ban from the mail anything he found to be "advocating or urging treason, insurrection, or forcible resistance to any law of the United States." Violators faced fines of up to $10,000 and as many as twenty years in prison under the law.

Postmaster General Albert Sidney Burleson

Beginning in the summer of 1917, Burleson ordered a ban on dozens of materials published by the American Socialist Party, including newspapers, the Socialist Party's *Appeal to Reason* and other magazines, journals, and letters that the postmaster found "offensive." With no way to distribute issues to their readers, many of these publications went out of business.

When anarchist publisher Max Eastman tried to mail out the August 1917 issue of *The Masses*, the post office blocked its distribution. One cartoon in the magazine depicted a boy strapped to the mouth of a cannon, which officials viewed as critical of the draft. When the

"AN EXCEEDINGLY DANGEROUS WOMAN"

Emma Goldman became one of the early targets of the antiradical campaign directed by President Woodrow Wilson during World War I. Goldman, at age sixteen, emigrated with her sister from Lithuania (at that time under Russian rule) to America in 1885 to escape a childhood marked by anti-Semitism, poverty, and an abusive father.

The 1886 Haymarket Square riot in Chicago, during which both police and protesters were injured, and the resultant trials, which condemned the anarchist leaders of the demonstration to death, inspired Goldman to join the fight against oppressive government. She embraced the anarchist cause, which rejected all forms of government authority and control. A passionate advocate for free speech, workers' rights, birth control, and women's equality, Goodman shared her vision in lectures given across the country, articles, essays, and her own literary and political magazine, *Mother Earth*. Thousands of people flocked to hear her speak in the early decades of the twentieth century. U.S. Attorney Francis Gordon Caffey characterized her as "a woman of great ability and of personal magnetism, and her persuasive powers are such to make her an exceedingly dangerous woman."

After the government banned *Mother Earth*, Goldman helped found the No-Conscription League, which sought to end the draft. She and fellow anarchist Alexander Berkman distributed pamphlets, went on lecture tours, and organized branches of the league in other cities. Police frequently disrupted the meetings.

Officials arrested Goldman and Berkman on June 15, 1917, on charges of interfering with the draft in violation of the Espionage Act. The jury rejected their claim that the First Amendment protected their speeches and writings. Berkman's impassioned question, in his own defense—"Are you going to suppress free speech and liberty in this country, and still pretend that you love liberty so much that you will fight for it five thousand miles away?"—failed to sway the jurors. The judge sentenced Goldman and Berkman to two years in prison and fined each of them $10,000. The U.S. Supreme Court upheld the lower court's ruling. After they served their sentence, J. Edgar Hoover, then director of the Justice Department's General Intelligence Division, ordered the couple's deportation to Russia.

Disillusioned with the Russian Revolution, Goldman and Berkman moved to Europe less than two years after their deportation. Goldman took an early stand against Adolf Hitler, the Nazis, and fascism. In later years, she continued her work as an anarchist in Canada. When she died, in 1940, the United States allowed her to be buried in Chicago near the bodies of the Haymarket anarchists. Thousands of people attended her memorial, where prominent speakers eulogized her dedication, courage, and idealism.

Emma Goldman (*left*) and Alexander Berkman. As a young man, Berkman served fourteen years in prison for his unsuccessful attempt to assassinate industrialist Henry C. Frick in 1892. The two anarchists were deported to Russia in 1919.

magazine's business manager asked officials to point out exactly what was objectionable, William H. Lamar, the U.S. Post Office's solicitor general, replied that "the entire tone and spirit" of the journal made it "unmailable."

Eastman appealed the ban, and the case went to court, making it the first court challenge of the Espionage Act. Judge Learned Hand of the New York State Superior Court ruled against censorship and for the magazine in a much-quoted 1917 decision. In analyzing the Espionage Act, Hand drew a fine line between "agitation"—speech that agitated for change—and speech that incited others to "violent resistance."

Political agitation, he noted, might in fact "stimulate men to violation of law." Nevertheless, he argued that democracies tolerated "all methods of political agitation," which "in normal times" was "a safeguard for free government." In his view, the Espionage Act—and the Constitution—allowed a man to criticize the draft but not to tell others specifically to break the law at a certain place and time. Although other courts would cite Hand's words in numerous future decisions, the U.S. Court of Appeals in a unanimous decision issued November 2, 1917, overturned his opinion and ruled against Eastman.

CHAPTER THREE

EUGENE V. DEBS AND THE ESPIONAGE ACT CASES

WITH THE NATION FULLY INVOLVED IN THE war effort, opponents to the war and the draft stepped up their efforts. In response, officials indicted those advocating resistance to the draft, stopped mailing privileges of magazines and flyers critical of the war effort, and increased actions against protesters. Opponents of the draft planned a massive march on Washington in 1917, but officials arrested 450 people involved in organizing the event before it could be held.

After America's draft law went into effect in 1917, 24 million men registered as required. Between 2 million and 3 million men refused to register for the draft and another 340,000 either did not report for duty after being drafted or deserted during training. Several draft-age men in Minnesota and New York refused to register. Lower courts convicted them under the Selective Draft Law. Their appeals eventually came before the Supreme Court as the *Selective Draft Law Cases*.

The men based their appeals on the claim that the Constitution had not empowered Congress to compel military service through a selective draft system. They further claimed that, even if the Court ruled that the Constitution had conveyed such authority to Congress, compulsory military service was "beyond the power" of Congress and "repugnant to the Constitution." The men wrapped their claims in the Thirteenth Amendment, which outlawed slavery and involuntary servitude. The draft, they argued, conflicted with the Constitution's guarantees of individual liberty.

On January 7, 1918, the U.S. Supreme Court ruled that the Selective Draft Law was constitutional. Chief Justice Edward D. White wrote the decision for the unanimous Court. In his opinion, the chief justice declared that Article 1 of the Constitution granted Congress the power to draft men into military service as part of its authority to "raise and support armies" and "to make all laws which shall be necessary and proper for carrying into execution the foregoing powers."

Chief Justice White asserted that to give Congress the power to form an army but not the means to provide men for that army "would seem to be too frivolous for further notice." He noted that while government had a duty to protect its citizens, citizens in turn had a reciprocal obligation to serve in the military to protect the government and the nation. The needs of the military might not always be fulfilled by voluntary recruits. In those cases, the federal government, not the states, had the power to enforce service in the military, White said. He pointed out that the United States had previously relied on the draft during the Civil War. In conclusion, White declared that the Court could not conceive of a theory under which the draft—requiring citizens to perform their "supreme and noble duty of contributing to the defense of the rights and honor of the nation"—would be a violation of the Thirteenth Amendment.

SEDITION ACT OF 1918

After Congress passed the Sedition Act of 1918, President Wilson signed it into law on May 16. The legislation, an amendment to the Espionage Act that toughened the government's stand against dissenters, made it illegal to use "disloyal, profane, scurrilous, or abusive language" about the government, the U.S. Constitution, military uniforms, or the American flag.

Attorney General Thomas Watt Gregory notified the U.S. attorneys charged with prosecuting federal law that "the prompt and aggressive enforcement of this

Act is of the highest importance in suppressing disloyal utterances and preventing breaches of peace." He also advised them, however, to use discretion when applying the law. "It should not be permitted to become the medium whereby efforts are made to suppress honest, legitimate criticism of the administration or discussion of government policies; nor should it be permitted to become a medium for personal feuds or persecution."

Despite this call for moderation, the federal government used the statutes to round up Socialists, anarchists, other radicals, and labor union members (particularly members of the Socialist labor union, International Workers of the World, or IWW), farmers, immigrants, and all types of people accused of criticizing the war and America's involvement in it.

Enforcement tended to be uneven. More zealous U.S. attorneys indicted anyone who even mentioned the war in a negative way, while other federal officials ignored all but the most pointed barbs against the government. Massachusetts, with a population of more than 3 million people, prosecuted only five suspects under the Espionage Act during the entire war. Western states, where the IWW concentrated its activities, had a much higher prosecution rate. For example, in sparsely populated North Dakota, with about 600,000 residents, officials brought 103 people to court for Espionage Act violations.

In one case, the government seized a film titled *The*

Socialists protest in Union Square, New York City. One sign reads: "The workers fight the wars. The bosses reap the profits."

Spirit of '76, which depicted Paul Revere's ride at the start of the American Revolution. The film was banned because it portrayed British soldiers as America's enemies. The moviemaker, Robert Goldstein, the son of a Jewish German immigrant, received a ten-year jail sentence. President Wilson later reduced the prison term to three years. In upholding Goldstein's sentence, a federal judge observed that the film might "make us a little slack in our loyalty to Great Britain."

Among those living in fear of the Espionage Act were German immigrants, many of whom had moved to the Midwest to set up farms and small businesses. Because the United States was at war with Germany, people of German ancestry came under suspicion as spies for the land of their birth. Neighbors, business associates, and acquaintances frequently reported German immigrants for making casual remarks about the war. This technique was used against Socialists and radicals as well. For example, associates pointed a finger at Fred Fairchild, a Socialist farmer in South Dakota, who said during an argument on the war that he would refuse to serve if he were young enough to be drafted. The remark earned him a year's sentence in Leavenworth Penitentiary for violating the Espionage Act.

In 1916 President Wilson set up the Council of National Defense and asked the states to establish their own councils. Originally intended to prepare the nation in the event of war, the councils coordinated war efforts after the United States entered World War I. In Montana, as in many states, the council's job was to protect the public safety and do what it could "toward the successful prosecution of [the] War." The Montana council's first task was to increase food production. Energies soon shifted, however, to boosting patriotism and suppressing dissent among the state's strong contingent of antiwar labor unions, radical farmers, and immigrants.

Once the United States entered the war, Montana passed legislation giving the councils of defense quasi-legal powers to bring charges against dissenters. District Attorney Burton K. Wheeler, one of the few public officials who spoke out against the system in Montana, said many of the cases brought to his office amounted to "feuds among neighbors who seized on the spy scare to try to

Immigrants disembarking from *Prinzess Irene* head to Ellis Island for processing.

settle old scores." People who voiced any complaint about the war or the government automatically faced suspicion. Rowdy gangs tarred and feathered residents who were reported to have expressed antiwar views or who refused to buy war bonds. Mennonite farmers, a pacifist religious group, eventually migrated to Canada after being harassed by self-proclaimed patriots.

Anti-German, anti-immigrant fervor rose to hysteria as legislators passed laws to ban German-language newspapers, local councils tracked down dissidents, schools discontinued German language classes, and newspapers peddled fear in headlines and news stories ("Are Germans to Bomb the Capitol City?" ran atop an editorial in the Helena *Independent*). Another editorial, printed several times in the Sidney, Montana, *Herald*, declared, "Every German or Austrian in the United States, unless known by years of association to be absolutely loyal, should be treated as a potential spy."

MONTANA AND THE COUNCILS OF DEFENSE

On March 6, 1918, traveling salesman Ben Kahn passed the time before breakfast chatting with the proprietor of the inn where he had spent the night in Red Lodge, Montana. The discussion turned to the war, then raging in Europe. "This is a rich man's war," Kahn complained to the innkeeper, T. F. Pollard. Pollard chaired the county council of defense (a fact Kahn was unaware of at the time). The wine salesman shifted his attention to state and federal regulations that restricted food consumption at home in order to feed U.S. troops and allies overseas. As part of the effort, Americans voluntarily observed "wheatless Wednesdays" and "meatless Mondays." "There's nothing to that, it's all a big joke," Kahn said.

Pollard responded with a chilly retort, "Well, if you feel that way about it, you must justify the sinking of the *Lusitania*."

"[The Americans] had no business in that boat," Kahn replied. "They were hauling over munitions and wheat."

An irate Pollard snapped back, "Anyone who says that is either a pro-German or an I.W.W. [member of the International Workers of the World labor union] or a damn fool."

After the exchange, Kahn visited several of his customers in town. By noon he had been arrested and charged with sedition. Convicted and sentenced to seven-and-a-half to twenty years in prison, Kahn served thirty-four months behind bars. He was one of seventy-nine Montana men and women who were convicted of violating the Espionage Act because they voiced opposition to President Wilson or the U.S. war effort during World War I. Many,

A poster distributed by the U.S. Food Administration during World War I encouraged Americans to abstain from eating wheat to provide enough to feed U.S. soldiers.

but not all, were German immigrants or first-generation Americans whose parents had emigrated from Germany.

The Montana Sedition Project, a website devoted to the state's citizens arrested in 1918 under the Espionage Act, aims to focus attention on that period in the state's history as a teaching tool for tolerance. "In our country," the project states, "the free exchange of ideas, which necessarily includes unpopular opinions, is at the heart of our democracy, and must be protected."

Governor Brian Schweitzer, at the request of the project's volunteers, issued pardons in 2006 for all seventy-nine Montanans convicted in the purge. "Across the country, this was a time when we lost our minds," the governor told the roomful of the convicted citizens' relatives during the pardoning ceremony. "It is time to say to an entire generation of Montanans 'We are sorry.' Send the word to the rest of the country. We may be first, but we shouldn't be last." Schweitzer, whose own grandparents were of Russian-German descent, was close to tears as he signed the pardons.

Hundreds of immigrants and other residents were indicted for offenses such as praising Germany, refusing to buy war bonds, criticizing U.S. policy, or complaining about "meatless and wheatless days." Officials indicted nine people for insulting the American flag, and another fifteen faced charges of being critical of war charity drives. In Tripp, South Dakota, thirty German-born residents were arrested for violating the Espionage Act after they signed a petition against the draft and sent it to the governor. North Dakota officials arrested Socialist Kate Richards O'Hare during a speech in which she declared that American women were "nothing more or less than brood-sows, to raise children to get into the army and be turned into fertilizer." Convicted of making a "seditious utterance," she received a five-year prison term. A Wisconsin judge, John Becker, lost his position and received a one-year jail sentence for saying that "it was a rich man's war and a poor man's fight." The judge was later cleared, but he never regained his job or his lost wages.

Officials prosecuted more than 2,100 people under the Espionage Act and the Sedition Act. As far as is known, not a single enemy spy was convicted under the act during America's participation in World War I.

"A FREE SOUL IN JAIL"

Among the most notable of the Espionage cases was one involving Eugene V. Debs, the Socialist Party's nominee for president in 1900, 1904, 1908, 1912, and 1920. Debs, a dynamic speaker, barnstormed across the country in 1917 and 1918, urging listeners to oppose America's participation in World War I and calling for an end to the draft. He gave one such speech to an enthusiastic crowd at the Ohio Socialist Party's state convention in Canton on June 16, 1918. That Sunday afternoon, Debs told his followers that he had just visited three Socialists imprisoned for speaking out against the war.

"I must be exceedingly careful, prudent, as to what I say, and even more careful and more prudent as to how I say it," Debs said to laughter from the audience. He acknowledged that officials might put "some of the rest of us in jail" for speaking out against the war. "But," he added, "I would rather a thousand times be a free soul in jail than to be a sycophant and coward on the streets." He assailed the United States' policy of jailing dissidents, in particular Kate O'Hare, who was in prison after her conviction for violating the Espionage Act. "The United States, under the rule of autocracy, is the only country in the world that would send a woman to the penitentiary for ten years for exercising her constitutional right of free speech," Debs declared.

After detailing Socialists' long history in opposing German autocracy, Debs urged the crowd to keep fighting against corrupt aristocracy and for the workers of the world. Socialists must fight "junkers" (aristocrats) everywhere, he said, in the United States as well as in Germany. "These very gentry, who are today wrapped up in the American flag, who make the claim that they are the only patriots, who have their magnifying glasses in hand, . . . are scanning the country for some evidence of disloyalty, so eager, so ready to apply the brand to the men who dare to even whisper opposition to junker rule in the United States."

Later in the speech, Debs claimed that wars were waged so that the ruling class could conquer and plunder the enemies' lands. The upper classes, he noted, always declared the wars and gained from them, while the working classes always fought the wars and had everything to lose, including their lives. He contended that rich Americans were making profits from wartime regulations of railroads, coal, food, and other commodities, while workers were laid off and citizens suffered from scarce resources. In a stirring conclusion, he urged the audience to join Socialists in their campaign for workers:

> We Socialists are the builders of the world that is to be. . . . We are inviting—aye, challenging you this afternoon, . . . to join us. Help do your part. In due course of time the hour will strike, and this great cause—the greatest in history—will proclaim the emancipation of the working class and the brotherhood of all mankind.

Eugene V. Debs ran on the Socialist Party ticket for president of the United States in 1900, 1904, 1908, 1912, and 1920.

The crowd signaled its approval with thunderous and prolonged applause. Other listeners, however, reacted far less approvingly. According to an account of the speech in the next day's issue of the *New York Times*, federal agents seized fifty-five young men in the audience who failed to produce draft cards on the spot. U.S. District Attorney Edwin S. Wertz told reporters he would take Debs's case before a federal grand jury if the Socialist leader had said, as reported, that the Allies had declared war for the purpose of plunder.

INDICTMENT AND CONVICTION

On Saturday, June 29, 1918, a federal grand jury indicted Debs on numerous charges arising from his June 16 speech. Socialists at the Bohemian Garden, where Debs was scheduled to address the crowd, immediately raised more than $1,000 (about $14,500 today) for his defense fund. The same day, Socialists in Indiana elected Debs as their nominee for U.S. Representative from the fifth district. The following day police arrested Debs in Cleveland, Ohio, and charged him with sedition under the newly approved amendments to the Espionage Act. The indictment included a laundry list of charges accusing Debs of

- making false statements "with intent to interfere" with military operations;
- attempting to aid enemies of the United States;
- inciting soldiers and sailors to mutiny and refuse to serve;
- attempting to obstruct the enlistment of men into the military;
- uttering "disloyal language" about the U.S. government;
- holding the government, the military, the flag, or military uniforms up to scorn and ridicule;
- speaking with the intention of inciting resistance to the United States and aiding its enemies;
- urging that production of war materiel be reduced;
- opposing the U.S. cause "by words."

During the trial, held in federal district court on September 11, 1918, in Cleveland, Debs acknowledged making the statements presented by the prosecution. His only defense rested on the right of free speech guaranteed by the First Amendment. Debs, tall and gaunt and wearing a worn gray suit, stood before the jury and said he would be willing to die in jail for his principles. "I would not take back a word of what I believe right to save myself from the penitentiary," Debs said. "I am accused of crime, but I look the Court in the face, I look the jury in the face, I look the world in the face, for in my heart no accusation of wrong festers." The Socialist leader observed that Abraham Lincoln and Daniel Webster had harshly criticized the administration of James K. Polk for waging the Mexican–American War. Prosecutors responded that the Espionage Act had not been in force then.

Judge D. C. Westenhaver ruled that the Espionage Act did not conflict with the Constitution. In giving his charge to the jury, the judge said, "The act was passed to protect the public peace and the public safety in time of war. The constitutional guarantee of free speech and a free press does not forbid the enactment of a law to protect the public peace and safety."

On September 12, after deliberating for almost six hours, the jury found Debs guilty on three counts of violating the Espionage Act. The guilty counts involved Debs's attempt to incite military men to mutiny and to refuse to serve; use of language intended to incite resistance to the United States and to promote the enemy's cause; and obstruction of recruiting and enlistment efforts. The jury found Debs not guilty of "opposing the cause of the United States." The judge instructed the jury to drop two other counts, and the prosecution did not present the remaining charges at trial. The conviction carried a possible penalty of twenty years in prison and a $10,000 fine on each of the three counts for which Debs was found guilty. On September 14 the former Socialist presidential candidate received a sentence of ten years in the federal penitentiary at Moundsville, West Virginia.

Debs appealed his sentence to the U.S. Supreme Court. At the request of the Justice Department, the Supreme Court agreed to expedite Debs's hearing and that of Jacob Frohwerk of Missouri, also convicted of violating the Espionage Act. Frohwerk, a Kansas City newspaper editor, ran afoul of the law for twelve articles he wrote denouncing U.S. participation in World War I. The articles appeared in the *Missouri Staats-Zeitung*, a newspaper catering to the German immigrant population. Like Debs, Frohwerk had been found guilty by lower courts, fined, and sentenced to ten years in prison. Oral arguments were scheduled before the Court for January 1919. The justices would hear the *Schenck* case first, however, and that decision would influence the outcome of others charged under the Espionage Act.

CHAPTER FOUR

BEFORE THE SUPREME COURT

THE U.S. SUPREME COURT AGREED TO REVIEW the case of Charles T. Schenck and Elizabeth Baer under a legal process called a writ of error. Under this procedure, the Court agrees to review a case to determine whether the trial court has made an outrageous error in law, as the person filing the appeal charges. In making its decision, the Court looks at the record of the trial to see if it was conducted correctly. The facts of the case are not reviewed. If the Court agrees that errors were made, the judgment is dismissed and the case is sent back to the lower court for a new trial. The writ of error was often used in appeals to the Supreme Court in the nineteenth and early twentieth centuries.

In today's Court, the writ of *certiorari* has replaced

The courtroom of the Supreme Court in the old Senate Chamber in the Capitol. The Court moved to its own building in 1935.

the writ of error. Appellants (people filing appeals) usually submit a petition for *certiorari* (meaning "to be informed of"). This document, a formal request for a hearing, briefly outlines the issues involved, lists the parties, and gives reasons why the Supreme Court should hear the case. The justices decide in a private conference which cases they will review. The Court hears only a small percentage of the petitions for *certiorari* submitted. In those cases where a petition is denied, the lower court's decision stands intact.

In the Schenck appeal, the Socialists' lawyers, Henry John Nelson and Henry Johns Gibbons, claimed that the judge erred when he allowed testimony on the Socialist Party's minutes, on the pamphlets, and on the newspaper clippings found in the Socialists' office. Such materials, they claimed, were confiscated illegally. They discounted the testimony of all the young men who received envelopes containing pamphlets because they argued that officials never proved that Schenck and Baer had anything to do with those particular mailings.

In addition, the lawyers contended that Baer's comments could not be considered at the trial because officials failed to warn her that her statements could be used against her. The judge erred, Nelson and Gibbons said, when he failed to instruct the jury to find the defendants not guilty and did not inform the jurors that the First Amendment protected speech and that people could be penalized only for harmful actions, not words. The judge also erred, they said, when he refused to grant the defendants a new trial.

Once the Supreme Court agreed to review the case, lawyers on both sides submitted briefs—a summary of arguments and previous cases supporting their point of view—to the Court. The justices scanned these papers when forming their opinion. Nelson and Gibbons outlined their case for Schenck and Baer in a thirty-one-page brief. John Lord O'Brian, special assistant to the attorney general for war work, presented the arguments for the United States. Alfred Bettman assisted him on the thirty-six-page brief. By the time the attorneys filed their briefs in December 1918, the war was over. On November 11, the allies signed an armistice with Germany, ending hostilities and sending cheering American soldiers home.

BRIEF FOR SCHENCK AND BAER

Nelson and Gibbons explored three questions in making their case for Schenck and Baer:

- Whether the First Amendment's guarantee of free speech rendered the Espionage Act unconstitutional;
- Whether there was enough evidence to convict the defendants;
- Whether the search warrant was constitutional and whether papers seized from the Socialists' office could legally be used as evidence against the defendants.

ESPIONAGE ACT VERSUS THE FIRST AMENDMENT

The Espionage Act, like its predecessor the Sedition Act of 1798, should be ruled unconstitutional, the brief stated, because of its chilling effect on speech and discussion. "How can a speaker or writer be said to be free to discuss the actions of the Government if twenty years in prison stares him in the face if he makes a mistake and says too much? Severe punishment for sedition will stop political discussion as effectively as censorship," the brief stated.

Nelson and Gibbons asserted that there was a distinction between words and acts. The First Amendment protected a man's right to say the draft law ought to be repealed but not his refusal to serve in the military after being drafted. "You don't have to put your hand into the fire because I tell you to do so," Nelson and Gibbons wrote, quoting an old adage.

The lawyers questioned how citizens could determine whether a war was just or unjust without "free and full discussion" on the topic. "Revolutions," they declared, "are not caused by freedom of expression." The brief cited a number of opinions issued in Espionage Act cases already decided by lower courts. The judge in one case, George M. Bourquin, had ruled that the Espionage Act was "not intended to suppress criticism or denunciation, truth or slander, oratory or gossip, argument or loose talk, but only false facts willfully put forward as true . . . with the specific intent to interfere with army or navy operations." To think otherwise, he said, was a "mistake." The judge noted that the Espionage Act required that "actual obstruction and injury" had to be proven, not just attempts to obstruct.

The brief quoted at length Judge Learned Hand's ruling in *The Masses* case. A review of such cases, the lawyers said in the brief, suggested that the First Amendment protected speech "made with sincere purposes to communicate honest opinion or belief." On the other hand, the First Amendment did not shield speech that masked "a primary intent to incite to forbidden action" and that actually resulted in illegal acts.

Judge Learned Hand

The lawyers noted that the Socialist circular did not incite illegal acts. Instead, it urged people to sign petitions to repeal the draft and quoted the words of U.S. Congressman Champ Clark, "A conscript is little better than a convict."

NOT ENOUGH EVIDENCE TO CONVICT

The lawyers argued that the sole evidence presented in court against Baer was the fact that she recorded the minutes of the executive committee's meetings. The prosecution provided "absolutely no further proof of any kind" that connected Baer to the alleged conspiracy, that she voted to distribute the circulars, or that she had even read the pamphlets. The brief went on to cite several rulings which established that "mere suspicion" was not sufficient grounds to convict a defendant of conspiracy. He or she had to be proven to have agreed to and participated in the plot.

In Schenck's defense, the lawyers contended that the prosecution did not prove that he conspired with anyone. "One person cannot conspire with himself," the brief stated. The minutes of the meetings, Nelson and Gibbons argued, should not have been allowed as evidence against their client. They noted that the prosecution provided no other evidence that the executive committee voted to circulate the pamphlet or that Schenck, a paid employee, participated in the voting. Nor, claimed the defense, did the prosecution present any evidence that Schenck himself mailed the circulars.

UNCONSTITUTIONAL SEARCH

The Fourth Amendment requires that officers must have probable cause before legally searching a person's premises, office, or other private area. Schenck's lawyers argued that the government violated that amendment when they searched the headquarters of the Socialist Party with no evidence of wrongdoing. Postal inspector Wynne failed to substantiate any suspected illegal acts when requesting the search warrant, the brief noted. In his testimony in court, Wynne did not name any witnesses to alleged illegal acts by the Socialist Party. He did not say what led to his belief that the Socialists were breaking the law. The brief also contended that the evidence seized in the search forced the defendants, indirectly, to provide testimony against themselves—a violation of the Fifth Amendment. However, the lawyers did acknowledge that some court rulings allowed written statements to be used against the authors.

Nelson and Gibbons asserted that the case was a political, not a criminal, matter. At the time the events took place, the Supreme Court had not yet decided on the legality of the draft law. The *Schenck* case, they said, presented a question of "human freedom," regardless of what the laws decreed or the Court ruled. "No government and no court and no law can easily afford to take issue with the smallest minority of citizens, if they . . . are steadfastly standing for what they honestly, conscientiously believe," the brief concluded.

BRIEF FOR THE UNITED STATES

O'Brian and Bettman, presenting the case for the United States, countered the *Schenck* brief with three arguments of their own:

- The Espionage Act was constitutional and consistent with the First Amendment.
- The prosecution presented enough evidence against Schenck and Baer for a conviction.
- The search warrant was constitutional.

The government's brief began with a detailed recap of events, including lengthy quotations of the disputed circular. The lawyers contended that the Socialists' conspiracy to persuade young men to evade the draft involved five "overt acts": approval of the plan, ordering the printing of the pamphlet, making arrangements for its circulation, mailing the pamphlet, and distributing it to the public at their offices.

CONSTITUTIONAL ESPIONAGE ACT

The Espionage Act prohibited the defendants' attempts to "cause insubordination, disloyalty, and neglect of duty in the military forces" and to "obstruct the recruiting and enlistment service"—and not their right to express opinions. Therefore, the case had nothing to do with the First Amendment, and the Espionage Act did not infringe on the defendants' free-speech rights, the brief stated.

Baer and Schenck clearly intended to incite young men to evade the draft, the lawyers said in their brief. The pamphlet itself illustrated that intent. It was not, as claimed, merely a recitation of opinion; it was a "frank, bitter, passionate appeal for resistance to the Selective Service Law." The fact that the mailings targeted young men eligible for the draft bolstered that conclusion, the brief asserted.

O'Brian and Bettman argued that most of the cases cited by Schenck and Baer's lawyers differed in important ways from their particular situation. They noted that the quotations from Judge Hand came from a case that the appeals court overruled.

Previous decisions of the Court already established the constitutional right of Congress to bar people from inciting men during war to illegally evade military service, the lawyers said. The brief cited three separate 1918 rulings, in *Goldman, Baker*, and *Ruthenberg*, that bolstered the government's case. In *Goldman* the Court ruled that a conspiracy did not have to produce successful results in order to be ruled illegal. In the other two cases the Court upheld the convictions of Charles Ruthenberg and Charles Baker, Ohio Socialists, for obstructing the draft.

SUFFICIENT EVIDENCE AGAINST THE DEFENDANTS

Both Schenck and Baer voluntarily identified the minutes of the Socialist Party meetings upon which the case was based, the government lawyers noted. They contended that it was up to the trial judge whether to admit certain evidence. The minutes showed that Baer was involved in the conspiracy, the brief stated. By her own testimony, she was the recording secretary for the local Socialist Party and wrote the minutes that detailed the conspiracy. Even if she were not involved, the lawyers argued that the minutes provided enough evidence to prove that Schenck was an active participant in the conspiracy, which also involved members of the executive committee and other "unknown persons" noted in the indictment. "There can be no reasonable doubt," the lawyers wrote, "that the action of the Executive Committee constituted the conspiracy."

CONSTITUTIONAL SEARCH

The lawyers maintained that the search warrant was legal, and that the evidence seized was within its scope. The government had probable cause for the search, the brief contended, based on the six hundred "seditious circulars" found at post offices throughout the city.

While defendants cannot be forced to testify against themselves, their written words can be used as evidence against them. The government's brief cited several cases—and the statements of the Schenck lawyers themselves—to support the claim that the judge was correct in allowing the minutes to be used as evidence in the trial.

THE JUSTICES

On Thursday, January 9, 1919, the justices assembled to hear the oral arguments in the case of Schenck and Baer. Following custom, the case became known by the name of the first plaintiff, *Schenck v. United States.*

Under Chief Justice Edward D. White, the Supreme Court in the second decade of the twentieth century took an active role in solidifying the conservative policies supported by the previous Court. Like its predecessor,

THE DISSENTERS: OLIVER WENDELL HOLMES AND LOUIS D. BRANDEIS

Justices Oliver Wendell Holmes Jr. and Louis D. Brandeis, from differing backgrounds and with divergent views, nevertheless formed a voting block on the Supreme Court.

Holmes came from a famous literary Boston family, fought for the Union in the Civil War (during which he was seriously wounded), served as chief justice of the Massachusetts Supreme Court, taught at Harvard Law School, and won respect in scholarly legal circles for his celebrated book on law. He was the oldest justice and had served on the Court for fourteen years when Brandeis was appointed in 1916. Tall and erect, with his handlebar mustache and white hair, he looked the part of an impressive and imposing member of America's intelligentsia.

Brandeis, the brilliant son of Jewish immigrants, never served a day as a judge before his appointment to the Supreme Court. He practiced law for more than thirty-five years as a champion reformer who created new ways to defend individuals' claims to constitutional rights against the property rights of corporations. Some viewed him as a radical, and his unruly gray hair and deep-set eyes with the fire of passion contributed to that image.

Together the two justices led the crusade for social and economic reforms. Often the Court's other justices overruled Brandeis and Holmes, who expressed their views in powerful dissents that future Courts would use in their defense of reforms and individual

Justice Louis D. Brandeis

Justice Oliver Wendell Holmes Jr.

rights. The dissents became so commonplace that they gave rise to jokes about the two justices. A scene in the play *Of Thee I Sing* included the announcement of the birth of the First Lady's son, to which one character intones, "Brandeis and Holmes dissent."

Holmes believed that legislatures, as representatives of the majority, and not the courts, had the authority to write laws. That view led him to support progressive laws on labor, child welfare, and other issues, which legislatures of the time passed and which the majority of the Supreme Court overturned. He also stood with Brandeis as a defender of First Amendment rights.

A powerful and graceful writer, Holmes authored more than 1,000 majority opinions and 23 dissents as a member of the Massachusetts Supreme Court and an additional 873 opinions, 72 dissents, and 30 concurrences during his long career on the Supreme Court bench. In his later years, Holmes became an icon to young legal professionals and others as a great judge rivaling John Marshall, the nineteenth-century chief justice who shaped the Supreme Court.

During nearly twenty-three years on the Court, Brandeis remained true to the progressive ideals he had practiced as an attorney. He voted in favor of minimum wages for women and children, upheld peaceful picketing by union members, and supported retirement benefits for rail workers. Scholars have praised his "brilliant defense of political dissent" in the 1927 case of *Whitney v. California* as "one of the most conceptually influential and rhetorically powerful justifications for First Amendment liberties."

Renowned for his scientific method of examining facts, Brandeis attracted a cadre of admirers—known as the "Brandeis men"—who practiced his way of thinking. A reporter once quoted him as saying he had no qualms about inviting a man with conservative views to tea as long as the man could think. "What I want to know is," Brandeis reportedly said, "is he intelligent?"

the White Court blocked measures passed by progressives in Congress and favored the rights of businesses over workers. Its rulings modified the antitrust laws to the benefit of monopolies, thwarted Congress's attempts to limit child labor, and rejected minimum-wage and minimum-hour laws. Justices Oliver Wendell Holmes Jr. and Louis D. Brandeis frequently opposed the majority decisions in stirring dissents that would form the basis of rulings by future Courts.

Among the Supreme Court's members were several prominent jurists. Legal experts place Holmes and Brandeis among the greatest justices ever to serve on the Court. Holmes served for almost thirty years, retiring at age ninety—the oldest justice in the Court's history. Brandeis had the distinction of being the first Jewish person to be named to the Court. White, a Democrat nominated by a Republican president, became the first associate justice to fill the chief justice's chair and one of only three Catholics to be named to the top position. Other members of the Court included Justices Joseph McKenna, William R. Day, Willis Van Devanter, Mahlon Pitney, James Clark McReynolds, and John Hessin Clarke.

ORAL ARGUMENTS

The nine justices, cloaked in black robes, sat at the imposing bench of the Supreme Court as the lawyers engaged in oral arguments. Nelson and Gibbons presented the Socialists' case to the justices. They argued several points. First, they contended, the government's case was weak because the prosecution had not produced enough evidence for a conviction. Second, officials did not have a valid search warrant when they collected the evidence the government did present in the trial. These technical points made little impression on the Court.

The main points of the arguments made on behalf of Schenck and Baer centered on their right of free speech and the importance of that right in the operation of a democracy. The First Amendment guaranteed the right of Baer, Schenck, and the Socialist Party to express their opinions on the war, the lawyers asserted. Even if the Socialists attempted to incite action against the draft with their words, the lawyers argued, they were expressing their honest views and beliefs—and the First Amendment protected such expression.

O'Brian, arguing for the government, contended that the executive committee's minutes, the pamphlets found in the Socialists' offices, and the letters and circulars mailed to draftees provided enough evidence to convict Baer and Schenck. The lawyer cited several cases, including the *Selective Draft Law Cases*, that backed his claim that Congress had the authority to pass laws, in this case the Espionage Act, to protect the country during war.

After listening to the lawyers' arguments over two consecutive days, the justices retired to their chambers to review the case on their own, discuss the merits of each side, and vote on the outcome. Traditionally, the chief justice expresses his views first, followed by those associate justices who wish to be heard. The justices then take a vote. If the chief justice votes with the majority, he assigns himself or an associate justice on the same side to write the decision for the Court. If the chief justice is in the minority, the associate justice on the majority's side who has served the longest on the Court makes the assignment. Justices who support the outcome but disagree with the reasoning behind it or who want to express their views on the case write concurrences, opinions that coincide with the majority vote. Those justices who vote against the majority may choose to write dissents, in which they state their reasons for opposition.

It can take several months or longer for a decision to be delivered in a particular case. There are no deadlines for decisions, except that opinions are usually issued on or before the last day of the Court's term (in late June or early July). In rare instances, justices may rehear a case if the membership of the Court changes before a decision has been rendered.

Two months would pass before the Court would issue its landmark decision in the Socialists' case, and Schenck and Baer would learn their fate.

Demonstrators dressed as pilgrims stand in front of the White House around 1919 with placards calling for the release of political prisoners, among them Socialist leader Eugene V. Debs.

CHAPTER FIVE

THE DECISION AND ITS AFTERMATH

ON MARCH 3, 1919, JUSTICE OLIVER WENDELL Holmes Jr. delivered the Supreme Court's decision in *Schenck v. United States.* The unanimous Court upheld the conviction of Charles Schenck and Elizabeth Baer and rejected their claim that the government had unconstitutionally interfered with their freedom of speech. Although the First Amendment protects freedom of the press and free speech, there are limits on those rights, the Court ruled. The Constitution allows the government, particularly in times of war, to protect the nation, even when those measures infringe on free speech.

The Espionage Act of 1917 made it illegal to interfere with the government's recruitment efforts. According to the Supreme Court, that was exactly what Schenck and his associates had done by circulating their pamphlet.

Justice Holmes acknowledged that "in ordinary times" Schenck and Baer "would have been within their constitutional rights" in mailing out the pamphlet to whomever they chose. Holmes noted, however, an action that might be perfectly acceptable during peacetime could endanger a nation at war. "[T]he character of every act depends upon the circumstances in which it is done," Holmes wrote. For example, he noted, the First Amendment's free-speech protections would not cover the words of someone "falsely shouting fire in a theatre and causing a panic. . . . The question in every case," wrote Holmes, "is whether the words used are used in such circumstances and are of such a nature as to create a clear and present danger that they will bring about the substantive evils that Congress has a right to prevent."

The Espionage Act, said Holmes, "punishe[d] conspiracies to obstruct, as well as actual obstruction." Even if there were no cases in which the pamphlet actually caused men to resist the draft, Schenck and his associates would still be guilty of conspiracy. The decision established that violators did not have to do any actual damage; their words merely had to exhibit a tendency toward harming the nation. Holmes's standard was based on "the bad tendency" test long established in English common law to punish subversive speech. Under the

Holmes test, the government could punish a speaker for speech that was intended to do harm even if the words did not ultimately cause any damage.

Holmes asserted that Schenck and his compatriots clearly intended for the young men receiving their pamphlet to resist the draft. "[T]he document would not have been sent unless it had been intended to have some effect, and we do not see what effect it could be expected to have upon persons subject to the draft except to influence them to obstruct the carrying of it out."

The nation had a right and a responsibility to protect its citizens from harm. That trumped an individual's free-speech rights, but only, Holmes said, under limited conditions. Holmes's description of the circumstances under which government can infringe on free speech—known as the "clear and present danger" test—became a benchmark in determining dozens of future cases.

The Supreme Court decision sent Charles T. Schenck to prison for six months at Mercer County Jail in Trenton, New Jersey. Baer served her ninety-day sentence at Philadelphia County Prison. They each were liable for a $500 fine.

His stint in jail did not deter Schenck from continuing his work for the Socialist Party. In 1920 he was one of 161 delegates attending the convention of the Socialist Party of America, held May 8–14 in New York City.

As a result of Baer's conviction for sedition, the

Pennsylvania Bureau of Medical Education and Licensure revoked her medical license for three months. She continued her work with the Socialist Party and was later quoted in the *American Labor Yearbook*: "Merely fighting the capitalist system should not be our aim. What is of far more consequence is that we educate the masses of workers. It is the power of knowledge that will triumph over the dark forces. If we can teach the truth to the people, they will free themselves."

DEBS AND FROHWERK

A week after delivering the *Schenck* decision, the Supreme Court issued similar rulings in the appeals of Eugene Debs and Jacob Frohwerk. Again the Court voted unanimously against the appellants, and, as in the *Schenck* case, Justice Holmes wrote the opinions. Although the Court did not specifically rule on the constitutionality of the Espionage Act, the rulings reconfirmed that the statute did not interfere with freedom of speech.

Debs, in making his appeal to the high court, had claimed that he had been prosecuted for his "state of mind." Holmes, however, asserted that Debs had intentionally tried to obstruct the government's efforts to recruit young men, a violation of the law. The justice said the Court had no interest in interfering with the parts of Debs's speech that focused on "Socialism, its growth and a prophecy of its ultimate success." He noted, though,

Debs's words lost the protection of the First Amendment when they encouraged listeners to obstruct the government's recruitment program.

The Court rejected Debs's contention that the judge had improperly instructed the jury at his trial. "[T]he jury was most carefully instructed that they could not find the defendant guilty for advocacy of any of his opinions unless the words used had as their natural tendency and reasonably probable effect to obstruct the recruiting service, . . . and unless the defendant had the specific intent to do so in his mind," Holmes wrote.

In ruling against Frohwerk, Justice Holmes declared that the First Amendment was never intended to provide protection "for every possible use of language." He stated, "We venture to believe that neither Hamilton nor Madison, nor any other competent person then or later, ever supposed that to make criminal the counseling of a murder within the jurisdiction of Congress would be an unconstitutional interference with free speech."

Noting that Frohwerk's articles used language very similar to that in the pamphlets distributed by Schenck, Holmes observed that the Supreme Court had already decided in *Schenck v. United States* that "words of persuasion" were enough to convict a person of conspiracy to obstruct recruitment. The justice acknowledged that there was no indication that Frohwerk made any attempt to contact men subject to the draft. Even so, Holmes wrote, the newspaper articles could have reached neighborhoods "where a little breath would be enough to kindle a flame, and that . . . fact was known and relied upon by those who sent the paper out."

In both cases, even though no evidence existed that the offending words led to violence or illegal acts, the *intent* to harm the nation was illegal under the Espionage Act. These two opinions reinforced the fact that Holmes's test included not only words that posed a "clear and present danger" but also words that showed a speaker's intent to cause harm. This has been termed the "bad (or dangerous) tendency test."

After the Supreme Court's decision in his case, Debs returned to the Atlanta Penitentiary where he was serving his ten-year sentence. There he conducted his fifth campaign for the presidency in 1920 from his prison cell. He managed to garner more than 900,000 votes as the Socialist Party's nominee, even more than he received in 1912, but only 3.4 percent of the electorate. President Wilson refused to commute Debs's sentence even at the urging of Attorney General A. Mitchell Palmer, a virulent anti-Communist who nevertheless believed Socialists like Debs—whom he put in a different category from Communists—did not deserve the harsh sentences meted out by the courts.

Communism, as espoused by Karl Marx in his 1848 book *The Communist Manifesto*, embraced Marx's view of a classless society in which everyone shared in the economic benefits of the nation. Unlike Socialists, however, Communists believed that it was necessary to overthrow the government to put workers in charge.

On Christmas Day in 1921, prison officials released the aging Debs on orders from newly elected president Warren G. Harding, who had pledged to return the country to normalcy during the 1920 campaign. A thousand prisoners cheered as Debs, using a cane, stepped outside the penitentiary gates after serving two and a half years. He died five years later.

Frohwerk had begun serving his ten-year prison sentence on June 29, 1918. After the Court's ruling, President Wilson commuted his sentence to one year.

A MARKETPLACE OF IDEAS

Another Espionage Act case, this one involving Russian immigrants, caused Holmes to rethink his "clear and present danger" test. The case, on appeal by Jacob Abrams, began in August 1918, as the war neared an end. In a sequence of events reminiscent of the Schenck episode, Abrams, a young anarchist, and four colleagues, all of whom had emigrated from Russia, were arrested as they distributed flyers in New York City. The pamphlets denounced the U.S. invasion of Russia after that country, under Communist control, withdrew from the war and negotiated a truce with Germany.

One flyer encouraged workers to participate in strikes at plants manufacturing ammunition and other supplies needed to wage war. Addressed to workers in the ammunition factories, the flyer advised Russian immigrants in particular that they were "producing bullets, bayonets, cannon, to murder not only the Germans, but also your dearest, best, who are in Russia and are fighting for freedom."

The dissidents printed about five thousand leaflets in English and in Yiddish on a press Abrams had purchased and stored in a basement. The young protesters threw the pamphlets from the window of a business where one of them worked and secretly distributed others.

Officials charged the protesters with conspiring to "urge, incite and advocate" people to take action against the war by circulating leaflets that contained "disloyal, scurrilous and abusive language about the form of Government of the United States." The official indictments, based on the Espionage Act and Sedition Act amendments, charged that the flyers used language "intended to bring the form of Government of the United States into contempt, scorn, contumely and disrepute" and "intended to incite, provoke and encourage resistance to the United States in said war."

At trial the dissidents acknowledged that they had written and distributed the flyers. They contended, as Schenck had, that there was not enough evidence to convict them and that the pamphlets had been produced to lend aid to fellow workers in Russia. They also claimed that the materials and their actions were protected under the First Amendment and that the Espionage Act (together with the Sedition Act) violated the Constitution. The lower court convicted the dissidents and issued prison sentences of fifteen to twenty years. The appeals court upheld the convictions and sentences.

When the case came before the Supreme Court on October 21, 1919, almost eight months after the *Schenck* decision, Abrams and his cohorts presented arguments, including a claim of First Amendment protections, similar to those used by Schenck. Unsurprisingly, the Court rejected the arguments and upheld the lower courts' rulings when it delivered the decision less than one month later, on November 10. Relying on the "clear and present danger" test devised by Holmes in the *Schenck* case, the Court found that Abrams and his associates had printed the pamphlets "at the supreme crisis of the war" and that they had distributed them in "an attempt to defeat the war plans of the Government." Therefore, the Court concluded, they "obviously intended to provoke and to encourage resistance to the United States in the war."

The Court ruled in its 7-to-2 decision that the dissidents had intended to incite riots and revolution in America in order to stop military operations in Russia. In a majority opinion written by Justice Clarke, the

Court discounted claims that the dissidents had merely been trying to help their comrades in Russia. Clarke wrote that they had been trying to "defeat the war plans" of the U.S. government by calling for a general strike that would have paralyzed the factories producing arms for U.S. soldiers.

What was surprising about the decision was the dissent delivered by the author of the *Schenck* test, Justice Holmes. He argued that the standard he had set in *Schenck* should be applied under much more narrow circumstances than those found in the *Abrams* case. While reiterating that the test remained necessary to protect the nation from "certain substantive evils," Holmes urged restraint in infringing on the right of free speech.

Holmes proposed a slightly modified version of his original standard: First Amendment free-speech protections could be overcome only if words created a "clear and imminent [rather than present] danger" which produced "forthwith" (or immediate) evils that threatened the nation. The changes required a direct link between words and an immediate threat.

In the *Abrams* case, Holmes observed, no one could suppose that a "silly leaflet" published secretly by an "unknown man" would "present any immediate danger" to the nation. He believed that the dissidents "had as much right to publish [two of the leaflets] as the Government has to publish the Constitution of the United

States." Even if he were wrong, Holmes said, the sentence of twenty years in prison suggested that the dissidents were being punished for their beliefs, not for the charges listed in the indictment. In the *Abrams* case, he noted, the dissidents' views on anarchy were examined at the trial, which should not have been allowed. "No one has a right even to consider [a person's system of belief] in dealing with the charges before the Court," he said.

Rather than barring dissent, Holmes said, it was far better, and more effective, to allow people to judge ideas for themselves and discard the ones they dislike. "[T]he best test of truth is the power of the thought to get itself accepted in the competition of the market." The founders based the Constitution on that theory, he said.

Concluding his plea for freer speech, Holmes cautioned his fellow justices to act only in true emergencies when making any exception to the First Amendment's directive, "Congress shall make no law . . . abridging the freedom of speech." He said, "We should be eternally vigilant against attempts to check the expression of opinions that we loathe and believe to be fraught with death, unless they so imminently threaten immediate interference with the lawful and pressing purposes of the law that an immediate check is required to save the country."

What led to Holmes's surprising change of heart in the nine months since the *Schenck* decision? One theory, posed by Cornell University history professor Richard

Polenberg and others, suggests that Holmes responded to criticism of his original "clear and present danger" test. In an article published in the *Harvard Law Review* in June 1919, Harvard history professor Zechariah Chafee had urged the Court to set a stricter standard when considering free-speech cases. During the Court's recess that summer, Holmes met with Chafee and corresponded with several other legal experts, including Learned Hand, the New York judge who had ruled against censorship in *The Masses* case in 1917. Following their discussion of the First Amendment and free speech, Holmes wrote his dissent calling for a stricter standard of judging First Amendment cases.

Despite his eloquent argument for a more rigid test, Holmes failed in persuading his fellow justices of its necessity. Only Justice Brandeis, who concurred with Holmes's dissent in the *Abrams* case and cast the only other vote in favor of the dissidents, supported the more stringent standard.

POLITICAL UPHEAVAL

Communists seized control of Russia in October 1917, withdrew from the war against Germany, and fought a civil war against forces supporting the tsarist government. The Allies viewed the Communists' withdrawal and subsequent treaty with Germany as an enemy act. In August 1918 the Allies, including the United States, sent troops to support the tsarist forces. Under pressure from home to end hostilities, all the Allied troops except the Japanese withdrew from Russia by 1920.

In the years after World War I, many Americans feared a Communist takeover as Russia gained power. Social unrest in the United States during this time increased Americans' apprehension. Union members, some of whom had links to the Socialist Party or to American Communism, went on strike across the country, demanding better working conditions and higher pay. The passage of Prohibition led to a crime wave fueled by profits from the illegal sale of alcohol. Race riots in Chicago, Omaha, and other cities left hundreds injured and thousands homeless, while the Ku Klux Klan lynched black Americans in a resurgence of violence. The 1918 flu epidemic, which killed 50 million people worldwide, added to the general agitation.

In the summer of 1919, a series of bombings rocked Washington, D.C., and seven other cities. The bombs were mailed to prominent politicians, editors, and other public figures who had taken stands against radical dissidents. Among the buildings damaged was the Washington home of Attorney General Palmer. The bomb at Palmer's residence was linked to Philadelphia anarchist Carlo Valdinoci, who officials later said was killed in the blast. Police never solved the other attacks, but officials, including future FBI director J. Edgar Hoover, who

Officials inspect the home of Attorney General Alexander Mitchell Palmer in Washington, D.C., after it was bombed by anarchists in 1919.

headed the investigation, blamed the bombings on a network of U.S.-based anarchists. The bombings intensified the already heightened fears of the American public.

Those fears led to the "Red Scare," a period after World War I during which dissidents of all types, but particularly Communists (whose red flag inspired the name) and foreign-born dissidents, came under suspicion. Officials, at the urging of Attorney General Palmer, stepped up their crackdown on dissidents. In a blistering article on American Communists written in 1920,

Palmer described the "Reds" as "criminal aliens," robbers, and murderers. He warned that the Communists' message of revolution had spread quickly across the nation, "eating its way into the homes of the American workmen, its sharp tongues of revolutionary heat . . . licking the altars of the churches, leaping into the belfry of the school bell, crawling into the sacred corners of American homes, seeking to replace marriage vows with libertine laws, [and] burning up the foundations of society." He believed that the actions of the dissidents put the U.S. government in jeopardy and argued for quick action against them even if no proof of actual crimes could be found. "There could be no nice distinctions drawn between the theoretical ideals of the radicals and their actual violations of our national laws," he wrote.

Technically the Sedition Act applied only during wartime. But officials extended the statute's reach by insisting the nation was at war because the United States still had troops in Russia. A report filed by the attorney general confirmed that 877 Americans were convicted of violations under the Sedition Act and similar federal laws between 1919 and 1920. Other sources placed the figure in the thousands.

In addition, local and state lawmakers passed their own peacetime antisedition acts and similar laws and ordinances. New York State operated its own raids under orders from the Lusk Commission, established by the

A drawing depicts the assassination of President William McKinley by Leon Czolgosz at the Pan-American Exposition, Buffalo, New York, in 1901.

legislature in 1919 to fight "seditious" activities. The New York police raided suspected radical headquarters, confiscated materials, and arrested dissidents under that state's criminal anarchy statute. The legislature passed the law in 1902 after the assassination of President William McKinley in New York in 1901. The assassin, Leon Czolgosz, was a self-professed anarchist whose parents had emigrated from Prussia (part of Germany).

In 1920 the New York legislature ejected five members elected on the Socialist Party platform. They were denied their rightful seats because the other assembly members viewed Socialists as "unloyal citizens." In a similar move, Congress refused to seat Victor Berger, a Wisconsin Socialist, in 1919 and again in 1920 after he won election to the House of Representatives. Berger, who with Debs helped form the Socialist Party of America, was sentenced to twenty years in prison under the Espionage Act for his antiwar statements, but the Supreme Court later overturned the conviction.

The Justice Department's special antiradical division, headed by Hoover, collected a dossier of information on dissidents and radical organizations so extensive that it filled 200,000 file cards. In December 1919 federal authorities herded 249 foreign-born dissidents, including anarchist Emma Goldman, onto a ship and deported them to the Soviet Union. In subsequent raids Palmer's men targeted members of the International Workers of the World, Communists, anarchists, and other left-wing groups and tried to drive them out of existence. During these so-called Palmer Raids, thousands of people whose only offense was to complain about the government were rounded up, arrested, and in some cases, sent to prison. The actions helped decimate the Socialist and Communist movements in the United States.

Partly in reaction to these abuses, Congress resisted efforts to pass an even tougher antisedition bill requested by the Wilson administration and eventually repealed the Sedition Act. In December 1920 the House approved a joint resolution that invalidated all laws that were to have ended upon "termination of the present war." The Senate added language to the measure that repealed the Sedition Act specifically but allowed the rest of the Espionage Act to be "revived and restored with the same force and effect as originally enacted." An amendment stipulated that the resolution would not affect the cases of people then facing charges or already convicted under the Sedition Act. Congress passed the bill, as amended, and it went into effect on March 3, 1921.

GITLOW V. NEW YORK

One of the first postwar dissident cases to reach the Supreme Court involved Benjamin Gitlow's appeal of a conviction for criminal anarchy. Gitlow had served in the New York legislature after being elected by the Socialists in 1917. In July 1919 the radical socialist arranged for the printing of sixteen thousand copies of the "Left Wing Manifesto" to be published by *The Revolutionary Age*, a Socialist magazine for which he was the business manager. The manifesto provided a detailed account of the doctrine of the Left Wing Section of the Socialist Party, a more radical branch of the mainstream group, which eventually became the American Communist Party. The radical group favored replacing the U.S. government with a new system giving workers more power. To achieve that goal, the group called for "mass political strikes" and "revolutionary mass action."

Shortly after the publication of the manifesto, New York police arrested Gitlow and Irish union organizer

James Larkin during one of their raids and charged them with violating the state's criminal anarchy law. The law made it illegal for anyone to speak, write, or publish words advocating anarchy, defined as "the doctrine that organized government should be overthrown by force or violence, or by assassination of the executive head or of any of the executive officials of government, or by any unlawful means." Violators were to be charged with committing a felony and subject to prison sentences up to ten years and fines of up to $5,000.

The magistrate who first ruled on the charges against Gitlow, William McAdoo, described the two as "mad and cruel men" and "positively dangerous men" for publishing the "revolutionary scheme" proposed in the manifesto. McAdoo also condemned all the members of the organization and anyone who "knowingly" subscribed to the publication. In his view, they were "equally guilty of violating" the state anti-anarchy statute.

Appearing before New York's trial court, Gitlow, twenty-eight years old at the time, faced two counts: advocating the overthrow of the U.S. government by force and ordering the printing of a publication that urged such an overthrow. Clarence Darrow, the famed civil rights lawyer, represented Gitlow during the trial in 1920. In his address to the jury, Darrow noted that no great revolution had ever been accomplished without force and violence. "Does that say I should not advocate a change, because somebody is going to get hurt?" he asked, adding, "Why, gentlemen, if that had been the law down through the ages and had been strictly enforced, you would all have been living in caves now." The fiery lawyer went on to quote Abraham Lincoln's first inaugural address in which he said that Americans could "exercise their constitutional right to amend . . . or their revolutionary right to dismember or overthrow" a government that no longer pleased them. Darrow observed that if Lincoln had uttered those words in 1919, Attorney General Palmer "would send his night-riders to invade his office and the privacy of his home and send him to jail."

Clarence Darrow

At the conclusion of the trial, Gitlow addressed the jury and delivered a fifteen-minute speech on his beliefs and on communism versus capitalism. The judge interrupted him several times and eventually barred him from speaking further. The prosecutor said of Gitlow, "He would make America a red ruby in the Red treasure chest of the Red Terror."

After deliberating for less than three hours, the jury found Gitlow guilty. He was sentenced to five to ten years in prison. The state's appeals court concurred with the lower court's ruling. Both courts upheld the constitutionality of the New York law, and the case went to the U.S. Supreme Court on appeal. After his conviction, Gitlow, a leader in the American Communist movement, began serving his sentence in New York's Sing Sing prison. In 1921, while still in jail, he ran as a candidate for mayor of New York City under the banner of the Workers' League, although city officials refused to place his name on the ballot. He was later released from prison while awaiting the Supreme Court's decision in his case. During this time, he ran as a candidate for vice president on the Workers' (Communist) Party ticket in the 1924 presidential race.

A FUNDAMENTAL RIGHT

John Caldwell Myers, assistant district attorney of New York, and W. J. Wetherbee and Claude T. Dawes, both Albany attorneys, presented the state's case. Walter H. Pollak, a New York lawyer and free-speech advocate, and Walter Nelles, one of the founders of the American Civil Liberties Union, made the case for Gitlow.

In his arguments before the U.S. Supreme Court, Pollak contended that the state government of New York had violated his client's rights based on the Fourteenth Amendment's due process clause. The clause bars states from making or enforcing "any law which shall abridge the privileges or immunities of citizens of the

United States; nor shall any state deprive any person of life, liberty, or property, without due process of law." The Supreme Court had ruled in an 1833 case, *Barron v. Baltimore*, that the Bill of Rights applied only to the federal government and not the states. But Pollak argued that the Court should overturn that ruling and that the states should not be allowed to infringe on a citizen's rights.

The Supreme Court heard arguments in the case on April 12, 1923. Lawyers reargued the matter on November 23, 1923. Since deciding the *Schenck* case in 1919, the Supreme Court had undergone a major realignment. By the time the *Gitlow* decision was finally delivered, five justices had died, retired, or resigned from the Court, and former president William Howard Taft had replaced Edward White as chief justice.

The Court issued its ruling on the *Gitlow* case on June 8, 1925. As in *Abrams*, the Court in a 7-to-2 vote upheld the conviction and the law. It was perfectly reasonable, the Court decided, for a state to try to protect itself from violent overthrow. Justice Edward Terry Sanford, newly appointed in 1923, delivered the opinion for the Court. Justices Holmes and Brandeis dissented.

In one remarkable and noteworthy sentence, the Court acknowledged Gitlow's argument that the Fourteenth Amendment applied to the states and that freedom of speech and freedom of the press were among the "fundamental personal rights and 'liberties'" protected under the due process clause. This statement, for the first time, established that states had to abide by the Bill of Rights and if their laws violated the rights spelled out by the Constitution, then the Court would overturn them.

By allowing the Fourteenth Amendment to be used in this way (called the incorporation doctrine), the Court provided citizens a tool to protect their rights against illegitimate state action.

Under the incorporation doctrine, the states as well as the federal government cannot infringe on citizens' fundamental rights without strong justification. In addition to the right of free speech and a free press guaranteed on the state level by the *Gitlow* decision, later Court rulings would apply other fundamental freedoms to the states, including freedom of religion and assembly, freedom against unwarranted search and seizures, the right not to incriminate oneself, and the right to a fair and speedy trial. *Gitlow*'s recognition of the incorporation doctrine would later lead the way for the great landmark cases of the Earl Warren Court, which used the doctrine to invalidate state laws that deprived black Americans, accused criminals, and others of their fundamental rights.

The ruling did not help Gitlow, however. Even with the First Amendment, Justice Sanford wrote, the Constitution does not grant citizens an "absolute right to speak or publish, without responsibility, whatever [they] choose." Nor does the Constitution prevent the government from punishing those who abuse their right to free speech, he said. "Reasonably limited, . . . this freedom [of speech] is an inestimable privilege in a free government; without such limitation, it might become the scourge of the republic," Sanford declared.

The majority relied on the "bad tendency" doctrine in reaching its decision. Sanford wrote that the Constitution allows states to ban an entire category of speech and publications which they find dangerous—for example, statements that advocate anarchy or Communism—as long as the laws are not unreasonable. This applies, the Court ruled, even when, as in the *Gitlow* case, the defendant did not advocate a "definite or immediate act" of "force, violence or unlawfulness" and did not encourage a particular person or group to break the law. The only requirement set by the Supreme Court was that Gitlow advocated such acts "in general terms" and that his language met the definition set in the law.

HOLMES AND BRANDEIS DISSENT AGAIN

Justice Holmes's dissent, joined by Justice Brandeis, has become a beacon for free-speech advocates. Although Holmes failed to sway the justices voting against Gitlow, other justices and other Courts have used his eloquent words to defend free speech and freedom of the press.

Returning to the test he first described in *Schenck*,

Holmes asserted that Gitlow's words fell far short of creating a "clear and present danger." The small minority of people who shared Gitlow's views could not rationally be seen as a threat to the government, the justice said. He discarded the claim that the manifesto itself was enough of an incitement to violate the law.

"Every idea is an incitement," Holmes wrote. "It offers itself for belief and if believed it is acted on unless some other belief outweighs it or some failure of energy stifles the movement at its birth. The only difference between the expression of an opinion and an incitement in the narrower sense is the speaker's enthusiasm for the result. Eloquence may set fire to reason."

He reiterated that Gitlow's words had no chance of igniting a revolution. The case might have been different, he said, if the manifesto had laid out a plot to overthrow the government in the immediate future. Some people might detest the Communist doctrine, but if the majority of Americans eventually adopted the ideas espoused in the manifesto, Holmes said, "the only meaning of free speech is that they should be given their chance and have their way."

In November 1925 Gitlow returned to prison to serve the remainder of his term. New York governor Al Smith granted his request for a pardon a month later. Declaring that Gitlow had been convicted of a "political crime," Smith said he believed the prisoner had been "sufficiently punished." He added, "I am satisfied that the ends of justice have been met and no additional punishment would act as a deterrent to those who would preach an erroneous doctrine of Government."

Gitlow immediately resumed his appeal to workers' groups and others to overthrow America's capitalist government and replace it with a Communist system. He sought the New York governorship in 1926 and again ran unsuccessfully for vice president in 1928. After internal upheavals among the American Communists, Gitlow lost his prominence in the party and later renounced Communism altogether.

WHITNEY V. CALIFORNIA

In 1927 the Supreme Court ruled on yet another free-speech case, *Whitney v. California*. As in *Gitlow*, the Whitney case involved a state statute that made speech itself a crime. This time Justices Brandeis and Holmes voted with the majority in affirming the conviction of Anita Whitney, who had been convicted of violating California's Criminal Syndicalism Act. The act barred "criminal syndicalism," defined as any doctrine "advocating, teaching or aiding and abetting" a crime, sabotage, or unlawful acts of force and violence. She was convicted of a felony for helping organize the Communist Labor Party in California, being a member of the organization, and attending the group's meetings.

While upholding the conviction, a concurring opinion written by Justice Brandeis and joined by Justice Holmes called for a much more stringent test when punishing speech. In this, as in *Abrams* and *Gitlow*, the two justices objected to the majority's view that words could be punishable even if they were unlikely to result in an immediate and violent act.

In his concurrence, Brandeis wrote an oft-quoted description of the importance of preserving free speech in a democracy. The country's founders "believed that freedom to think as you will and to speak as you think" were "indispensable" to discovering the truth. "[P]ublic discussion is a political duty, and . . . this should be a fundamental principle of the American government."

The justice asserted that "fear of serious injury" is not enough to justify infringement on free speech. "Men feared witches and burnt women," he said, referring to the Salem witch trials of the seventeenth century. Free speech, he said, can conquer irrational fears. Laws that interfere with free speech, therefore, must be based on reasonable grounds that the words uttered will result in a "serious evil." In addition, Brandeis stated, there must be reasonable ground that the danger will be imminent. Even if a person advocates that a law be broken or that his or her speech "is likely to result in some violence or in destruction of property," that is not enough to justify infringing on free speech if the words do not incite others to take immediate illegal and violent action, Brandeis wrote. "In order to support a finding of clear and present danger," he said, "it must be shown either that immediate serious violence was to be expected or was advocated, or that the past conduct furnished reason to believe that such advocacy was then contemplated." Only in an emergency, when there is no time for rational discussion to dispel the violent ideas being introduced and there is an immediate threat of serious harm to the state should government have the power to put limits on speech, Brandeis said.

In reviewing the Whitney case, Brandeis said the California law met constitutional muster because it was based on "the immediate preservation of the public peace and safety." However, he noted, the law may have been applied erroneously in cases where a person's speech did not result in a "clear and present danger." Brandeis observed that Whitney could have defended herself against the charges by proving that her words had no "bad tendency" to do immediate harm and that no "serious evil" or imminent danger would have resulted from her words. Since she failed to do so and the prosecutor presented evidence that the Communist group's activities encouraged serious crimes by members of the International Workers of the World, the high court had no choice but to uphold her conviction.

CHAPTER SIX

SAFETY VERSUS FREEDOM

IN THE YEARS THAT FOLLOWED, PEOPLE WHO spoke their minds continued to get into trouble with the law. Courts in time began to lean toward allowing speakers more freedom. Some decisions relied on the stricter application of the "clear and present danger" standard as outlined in the opinions of Justices Oliver Wendell Holmes and Louis D. Brandeis.

In a 1941 case, *Bridges v. California*, a divided Court ruled that a union leader's telegram to a judge did not present enough of a "clear and present danger" to justify restricting his speech. Justice Hugo Black, who wrote the majority opinion, asserted that having "an inherent tendency" or "a reasonable tendency" to cause harm was not enough to interfere with freedom of speech. California's law, he said, effectively censored any public commentary on a pending court case. That, in his view, could not be dismissed as an "insignificant abridgment of freedom of expression." Black added that "it is a prized American privilege to speak one's mind, although not always with perfect good taste, on all public institutions." In subsequent decisions, however, the Court ignored Black's reluctance to infringe on free expression based only on a "tendency" to cause harm.

CENSORSHIP MAKES A COMEBACK

During the years leading up to World War II and the cold war that followed, when Americans once again feared a Communist takeover, laws censoring speech made a comeback. In 1940 Congress passed the Alien Registration Act as a response to President Franklin D. Roosevelt's warning that "spies, saboteurs and traitors" threatened national security. A provision of the bill, known as the Smith Act after its author Representative Howard W. Smith of Virginia, made it illegal to advocate or conspire to advocate the violent overthrow of the government. The broad sweep of the law applied to speakers, publishers, teachers, groups, and anyone else who espoused such ideas. Punishment for violating the law included fines and prison sentences up to twenty years.

In 1951 the Supreme Court, by a 6-to-2 majority, upheld the Smith Act in *Dennis v. United States*, and affirmed the convictions of eleven Communist Party leaders. The case involved Eugene Dennis, general secretary of the Communist Party in the United States, and ten other Communist leaders, including Gus Hall, who later ran for president of the United States. They were charged with advocating the overthrow of the government with force and violence, in violation of the Smith Act. Officials based the charges on the men's organization of the Communist Party, which had as part of its doctrine the goal of overthrowing the U.S. government. During oral arguments before the Court, their lawyers protested that the prosecutions amounted to "an unabashed suppression of political ideas that were thought dangerous." The decision left in place fines of $10,000 each and five-year prison terms for all but one man, whose sentence was reduced to three years in light of his exemplary military service during World War II.

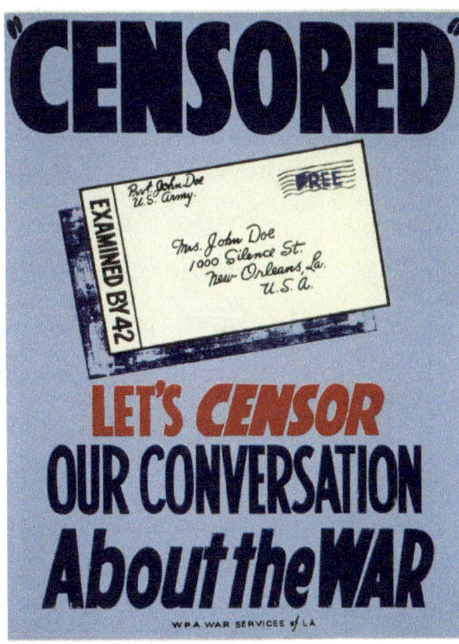

Government-issued posters warned Americans not to talk about World War II.

Chief Justice Fred M. Vinson's majority opinion asserted that, by organizing, the Communists had entered into a conspiracy that created a "clear and present danger" to the government. Although the Court reiterated support for the Holmes test, the majority did not require that the plot be imminent, as

Holmes had stipulated in the *Abrams* dissent, or require evidence that the attempt would be successful. In fact, the Court ruled, merely advocating for a violent doctrine was enough to justify infringement on free speech. Vinson wrote that the government was justified in acting before a plot to overthrow it could be executed.

Justice Black and Justice William O. Douglas filed separate dissents in the case. Black charged that the majority had repudiated Holmes's "clear and present danger" standard and in doing so had greatly restricted First Amendment protections. He observed that the defendants had not been charged with any acts or even any words that indicated they meant to overthrow the government. The Smith Act, he said, was "a virulent form of prior censorship of speech and press, which I believe the First Amendment forbids."

Justice Douglas presented similar views in his passionate defense of the First Amendment. He said that the First Amendment did not require the government to take no action while Communists taught "the techniques of sabotage, the assassination of the President, the filching of documents from public files, the planting of bombs, the art of street warfare, and the like." The defendants in the case, however, were not charged with such things; their offense was to organize people to teach the Communist doctrine.

"Seditious conduct can always be punished," Douglas

observed. "But the command of the First Amendment is so clear that we should not allow Congress to call a halt to free speech except in the extreme case of peril from the speech itself." Noting that most Americans would cheer the majority decision given the political climate of the country (during the cold war), Douglas nevertheless expressed hope that "in calmer times, when present pressures, passions and fears subside, this or some later Court will restore the First Amendment liberties to the high preferred place where they belong in a free society."

BRANDENBURG: A NEW STANDARD

That is exactly what happened when the Supreme Court under Chief Justice Earl Warren overturned the *Whitney* ruling in 1969. In a unanimous decision in *Brandenburg v. Ohio*, the Court rejected the "bad tendency" test it had used in *Gitlow* and made it more difficult for the government to restrict speech. The Court's opinion set up a new, more rigorous standard that government must use to determine when speech does not merit First Amendment protection.

The case revolved around Clarence Brandenburg, a leader of the Ku Klux Klan (KKK) in Ohio. The organization was originally formed in 1866 to fight for white supremacy and against freed slaves. In the mid–1910s, the KKK re-formed and rapidly increased membership throughout the Red Scare until 1944, when the group disbanded in the wake of corruption among its leadership. It underwent a resurgence in the 1950s during the cold war amid the growing push for civil rights among black Americans. Members wore hooded white sheets and terrorized, tortured, and killed black Americans and their sympathizers. They later targeted Jews, Catholic immigrants, Socialists, and Communists as well.

In 1964 Brandenburg invited a television news reporter in Cincinnati to film a KKK rally at a nearby farm. The television footage showed twelve hooded figures gathered around a large wooden cross. The figures, some of whom carried firearms, set the cross on fire while muttering derogatory words about black Americans and Jews. In one scene, a man wearing a hooded white robe, identified as Brandenburg, spoke to the group, saying that "if our President, our Congress, our Supreme Court, continues to suppress the white, Caucasian race, it's possible that there might have to be some revengeance taken." He noted that the KKK, "four hundred thousand strong," would be marching on Congress on July 4.

On the basis of the film, part of which was broadcast on a national newscast, Ohio officials arrested Brandenburg and charged him with violating the state's criminal syndicalism statute. The law, enacted in 1919, resembled California's statute and made it a felony to "by word of mouth or writing advocate or teach the duty, necessity or propriety of crime, sabotage, violence or unlawful methods of terrorism as a means of accomplishing industrial or political reform." An Ohio jury found Brandenburg guilty, and the court sentenced him to ten years in prison and fined him $1,000. The state's higher courts rejected his appeal.

The U.S. Supreme Court heard arguments in the case on February 27, 1969. A team of prominent ACLU lawyers represented Brandenburg. For years the rights organization had been trying to overturn the criminal syndicalism laws and other antisedition statutes, which the ACLU believed violated the free-speech protections of the First Amendment. The *Brandenburg* appeal provided a test case in which the ACLU lawyers could present their free-speech arguments to the Warren Court.

The Court's rulings on two earlier cases provided hope to free-speech advocates. In the 1957 decision for *Yates v. United States*, the Court threw out the convictions of fourteen people accused of violating the Smith Act for advocating Communism and forming a branch of the Communist Party. The ruling noted the difference between advocating a general doctrine (even if the doctrine itself urged violent acts) and laying out a plan to actually accomplish the violent goals of the creed. "The essential distinction is that those to whom the advocacy is addressed must be urged to *do* something, now or in the future, rather than merely to *believe* in something." In the second case, *Noto v. United States*, decided in 1961, the Court reversed the conviction of a New York man similarly found guilty of Smith Act violations because of his speeches on Communism and membership in the local party. The justices reaffirmed their conclusions in *Yates* and ruled that "the mere abstract teaching of Communist theory, including the teaching of the moral propriety or even moral necessity for a resort to force and violence, is not the same as preparing a group for violent action and steeling it to such action."

On June 9, 1969, the Court delivered an unsigned, unanimous opinion overturning Brandenburg's conviction and ruling that Ohio's law and others like it violated Americans' free speech rights, protected under the First Amendment. The decision invalidated the Smith Act and the *Whitney* ruling. Justice William Brennan revamped an opinion written by former Justice Abe Fortas for the Court. Fortas was forced to resign over ethics questions before the Court delivered the decision.

In the opinion, the Court reworked the original "clear and present danger" test to bring it more in line with Holmes's later explanation of the standard in his *Abrams* dissent. Under the First Amendment, the Court ruled, states cannot punish speech that advocates breaking the law or using force "except where such advocacy is directed to inciting or producing imminent lawless action and is likely to incite or produce such action."

The brief opinion, which the ACLU proclaimed as

"one of its 100 greatest hits," established a new standard, referred to as the *Brandenburg* test. Under the new test, the government must prove three things to justify infringing on free speech:

1. The intention of the speaker is to incite or produce unlawful actions.
2. The words must result, or be seen as likely to result, in an illegal act or acts.
3. The threat of illegal actions must be imminent, or the actions must be expected to occur immediately.

Criminal syndicalism acts like Ohio's did not meet the test's requirements, the Court ruled. Instead, the Ohio statute sought to "punish mere advocacy" and to prohibit people from gathering together "merely to advocate" their cause. Such laws, the Court declared, violated both the First and the Fourteenth Amendments.

Justices Black and Douglas—among the Court's most ardent supporters of First Amendment rights—voted with the majority, but they both added concurrences that rejected the "clear and present danger" standard altogether. In his longer concurrence, Douglas noted the many forms Holmes's test had taken in Court decisions through the years and its use, in the *Dennis* case and others, to punish political dissidents for their words and acts of protest. Whether a young man burns his draft card in protest of the Vietnam War, an atheist shreds his Bible to celebrate his new views, or a citizen tears up his copy of the Constitution to protest a Supreme Court decision—all are forms of expression and all fall within the protection of the First Amendment, Douglas asserted.

"I see no place in the regime of the First Amendment for any 'clear and present danger' test," Douglas wrote, "whether strict and tight as some would make it, or free-wheeling as the Court in *Dennis* rephrased it." He criticized the line drawn by the Court "between the criminal act of being an 'active' Communist and the innocent act of being a nominal or inactive Communist." In Douglas's view, the First Amendment protections do not cover speech when a violent act is inseparable from the words uttered (such as in Holmes's example of a man falsely shouting "Fire!" in a theater and causing a riot). Otherwise, Douglas said, "speech is . . . immune from prosecution. . . . Government has no power to invade that sanctuary of belief and conscience."

In the years that followed, the Court relied on the *Brandenburg* test to decide several First Amendment cases. In the 1970s the Court applied the test to cases involving antiwar protesters, members of the Communist Party of Indiana, and famed pediatrician and presidential candidate Benjamin Spock, among others. Later cases addressed NAACP official Charles Evers's advocacy of a boycott in Mississippi (protected by the First Amendment) and flag burning as a protest (also protected). The dwindling number of cases involving inflammatory speech since the 1970s indicates the power of the *Brandenburg* test, attorney and law journal editor Christopher M. Montgomery says. Its existence has discouraged officials from clogging the courts with speech-related cases because they know most examples will not meet the test.

Lower courts have also used the *Brandenburg* test in a number of cases, including those related to terrorist suspects. One case, decided in federal court in Idaho in 2004, involved a Saudi computer student named Sami Omar Al-Hussayen. The government charged him with advocating "extreme jihad" (a holy war) via the Internet. He also faced charges of fraud and aiding terrorists. The government maintained that he used his computer skills to recruit and raise money for an Islamic organization suspected of aiding Middle Eastern terrorists and for Hamas, a Palestinian extremist group. At trial,

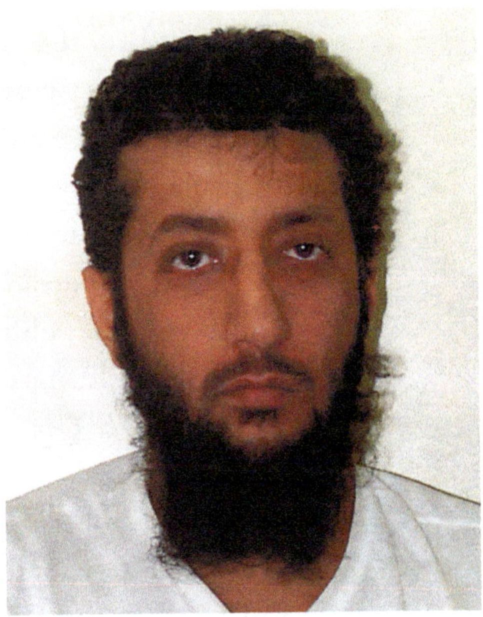

Sami Omar Al-Hussayen

government prosecutors argued that Al-Hussayen had incited others to engage in a holy war against the United States. The defense team cited the *Brandenburg* ruling in its claim that their client's words were unlikely to result in "imminent lawless action." After the jury found him not guilty of most of the charges, prosecutors negotiated a deal to drop the remaining charges if Al-Hussayen did not appeal his deportation. He was deported to Saudi Arabia following his release from jail. Critics of the *Brandenburg* test point to that case in their arguments for a different standard that is less protective of free speech for terrorism cases.

A CONTINUING BALANCING ACT

The balancing act between protecting free speech and ensuring national security continues to challenge Americans in the twenty-first century. "Terrorism presents a special challenge to a democratic society: how to prevent and punish ideologically motivated violence without infringing on political freedoms and civil liberties," wrote James X. Dempsey and David Cole in their book *Terrorism and the Constitution: Sacrificing Civil Liberties in the Name of National Security*.

Critics of the *Brandenburg* decision question the ability of the test to address the complex issues when terrorism is involved. For example, Bruce Fein, a former official in the Justice Department under President

Ronald Reagan, observed that *Brandenburg*'s "imminent" requirement forces courts to condemn a man who lights a fuse designed to set off an explosion in five minutes while excusing a man who ignites a fuse that takes five weeks to go off.

Conservative commentator Richard Miniter contends that the *Brandenburg* standard has made it difficult to prosecute foreign terrorists. "Today, *Brandenburg* safeguards those who inspire terrorists with their words," he writes. "Today, *Brandenburg* protects terrorist recruiters who inspire their followers to train for a life of murder, and safeguards those who raise money for bombs to annihilate or disfigure civilians."

Another critic, Robert H. Bork, solicitor general under President Richard Nixon and judge in the U.S. Court of Appeals, believes the *Brandenburg* test illogically requires judges to decide the likelihood that certain words will result in violent acts. "The *Brandenburg* formula requires judges to estimate such matters as the danger posed by an al Qaeda leader's call for jihad [holy war] in America, or the mood of a crowd hearing incitement to racial violence," Bork wrote in a letter to the editor of *Commentary* magazine, in 2005. "These are tasks for which the judiciary is the least qualified branch of government."

During his term of office, George W. Bush repeatedly pushed for new rules to fight the war on terror.

Faced with the violence of the September 11 attacks and threats from Islamic extremists, members of the Bush administration and others argued that the nation needed to be able to gag advocates of terrorism to protect Americans. Even defenders of the *Brandenburg* test acknowledge that it may run into difficulty in times of war or when applied to terrorist plots or the use of the Internet by advocates of violence. While *Schenck* pertained to a wartime case, *Brandenburg* concerned a domestic matter not related to war.

In light of modern-day challenges, First Amendment scholar Ronald Collins sees value in an expanded version of the Holmes test proposed by Richard Posner, a judge on the U.S. Court of Appeals. That approach would weigh a number of factors, including the benefits of the speech, the costs of punishing such speech, the probability that the speech would produce harm, the type of harm produced, and the time between the speech and when the harm would be expected to occur. Under the Posner formula, speech could only be punished if its costs and the probability of harm outweighed its benefits.

The Internet has been a focus of concern among those who want to regulate communications between terrorists and a susceptible audience of listeners. Some have proposed that Internet service providers monitor their networks and report on suspicious postings. Some companies, at the request of the government, have already censored some clients' speech, a development that disturbs free-speech advocates. "The dangers of this arrangement are profound," writes Montgomery in an article published in the *Ohio State Law Journal.* Such censorship is likely to target speech that should be protected by the Constitution, Montgomery says.

Free-speech advocates argue that officials who claim terrorism requires more stringent control of inflammatory speech are no different from earlier leaders who punished Socialists for their views during the Red Scare or the seventeenth-century zealots whose fear of witchcraft led them to put women to death for their unorthodox views. "Governments are always claiming freedom of speech is dangerous," says Eric Foner, Pulitzer Prize–winning author and historian, in a 2009 documentary on freedom of speech titled *Shouting Fire: Stories from the Edge of Free Speech.* In the same documentary, Donna Lieberman, executive director of the New York Civil Liberties Union, says, "Don't they get it? In a democracy, you have lawful protest *instead of* terrorism."

As for those who say judges are unqualified to determine risk, law professor Geoffrey R. Stone responds, "The standard argument of the executive is that judges are not competent to second-guess military judgments about the demands of national security. But it is equally true that those who run the military are not competent to make difficult judgments about civil liberties."

In 2010 WikiLeaks, an online organization that publishes sensitive government documents on the Internet, posted more than 250,000 classified messages from U.S. officials to U.S. embassies around the world. The correspondence included information on the wars in Iraq and Afghanistan and on diplomatic relations with many other countries. The case has raised new questions about how to deal with the distribution of what many consider "dangerous" speech via the Internet.

U.S. officials have threatened to charge Australian Julian Assange, WikiLeaks's founder, under the Espionage Act of 1917, which is still on the books in modified form. U.S. Attorney General Eric Holder said the documents' publication "puts at risk our national security, but in a more concrete way it puts at risk individuals who are serving this country in a variety of capacities, either as diplomats [or] as intelligence [agents]. It puts at risk the relationships that we have with important allies around the world."

Assange's lawyer, Jennifer Robinson, said the Espionage Act did not apply to her client. "In any event," she said, "he's entitled to First Amendment protection as publisher of WikiLeaks, and any prosecution under the Espionage Act would in my view be unconstitutional and puts at risk all media organizations in the U.S."

Supporters of Assange hail him as a free-speech hero, while his detractors consider him to be a terrorist who

Julian Assange, outside the High Court in central London in December 2010, shows the paperwork granting him bail.

has aided America's enemies. The case could make its way to the Supreme Court for final resolution. Assange was under house arrest in England and fighting extradition to Sweden, where he was wanted on a sexual assault charge, when this book went to press.

Clearly, the First Amendment does not protect violent behavior. It does not bar the government from protecting the nation against harm, from terrorists, or other dangers. "When dissenters cross the line between peaceful dissent and violent conduct they shed the protection of the First Amendment. Assassination is not a First Amendment right," notes law professor Stone. But the Supreme Court has decreed that the line between words and immediate, illegal action must be crossed if officials are to press charges. As Justice Douglas wrote in his dissent in *Dennis*, a restraint on speech "must be based on more than fear, on more than passionate opposition against the speech, on more than a revolted dislike for its contents. There must be some immediate injury to society that is likely if speech is allowed."

A democracy cannot function without some element of risk. Citizens need access to information—even articles and words that some may consider dangerous or vile—if they are to fulfill their duties as watchdogs and overseers of a powerful government. If officials can punish expressive views they do not like without adhering to a rigorous test, then government can manipulate information and subvert the will of the people. That is when safety—measured by having no exposure to dangerous words—itself becomes a danger to the survival of democracy. "After two centuries of doctrinal evolution," says Stone, "we are willing to accept quite a bit of risk in order to guarantee a robust and wide-open political discourse, even in time of war."

First Amendment scholar Collins observes that risk is "the cost of real freedom." People who insist on being safe may pass laws that allow officials to punish certain speech, may "subject the Internet to broadcaster-like government regulations; always keep protestors a binocular distance from people in power; oppose press shield laws; outlaw 'dangerous' speech in wartime; . . . zone out free expression; and create more exceptions to the First Amendment." If that happens, he warns, "you will be very safe, but alas not free."

THE FIRST AMENDMENT

GUARDIAN OF FUNDAMENTAL RIGHTS

After the American Revolution, citizens set out to create a government for their new nation that would not duplicate Britain's abuses of power that led to war. The Constitution they adopted established a blueprint for the government's operations, while the Bill of Rights protected individual rights from interference by a powerful federal government.

Number one on the Bill of Rights, the First Amendment, guarantees individual Americans some of their most precious rights:

- Freedom to practice their own religious beliefs and a ban on a state religion that would receive preferential treatment over other faiths.
- Freedom to speak without fear of punishment by the government for expressing their views.
- Freedom for the press to publish without interference from the government.
- Freedom to meet in a peaceful manner and associate with whomever they choose.
- Freedom to protest against government actions and to join together to demand change.

In drafting the First Amendment, the founders recognized several principles of American democracy:

- People have a right to freedom (although black Americans were not granted this right until the Thirteenth Amendment abolished slavery).
- Democracy relies on the free expression of its citizenry. To make informed choices about government and their leaders, citizens must have access to a free flow of information. A free "marketplace of ideas" provides citizens with a variety of views and facts on which to evaluate candidates for public office and to assess their performance. Such freedom cannot exist if the government controls the information Americans are allowed to receive.
- The government (and Congress's laws) must not interfere with Americans' basic rights. However, the courts have allowed government to regulate fundamental rights, including freedom of speech, under certain circumstances.
- When rights conflict with each other, the courts must balance them to determine which one has priority. For example, extensive media coverage (freedom of the press) may have an impact on a person's right to a fair trial.
- The First Amendment applies to everyone. Americans are entitled to express their opinions or follow their religion even when other people find such views or religious practices to be offensive.

Since its ratification on December 15, 1791, the First Amendment has stood between Americans and attempts by overzealous moralists, self-promoting politicians, and overreaching officials to stifle dissent, muffle the media, intimidate members of unpopular groups, quell protests, and impose religious views on people whose beliefs are at odds with the majority. The First Amendment has been at the heart of dozens of U.S. Supreme Court cases involving religion or individual beliefs, protest, free speech, and freedom of the press.

The First Amendment often lies at the center of bitter disputes. Despite its lead position in the Bill of Rights, the First Amendment—or at least its interpretation by the courts—has frequently given rise to howls of protest. Does the guarantee of free speech apply to protesters who express their views by burning the flag? Does freedom of the press extend to pornographic magazines and films? Does freedom of religion mean that children cannot sing Christmas carols in public schools? The answers to those questions are not always clear, and court decisions in cases that arise from them are often controversial and unpopular.

Yet that is how a democracy operates. Disputes rage, courts issue rulings, and people use their First Amendment right to free speech to applaud or denigrate the results. It's a free country—in large part because of the protections that the First Amendment provides.

NOTES

INTRODUCTION

p. 10, "Congress certainly cannot . . .": *Abrams v. United States*, 250 U.S. 616 (1919).

CHAPTER ONE

p. 12, "A conscript . . .": Anastaplo, *The Constitutionalist: Notes on the First Amendment*, Lanham, MD: Lexington Books, 2005, 298–299.

p. 12, "Do not submit . . .": Anastaplo, *The Constitutionalist: Notes on the First Amendment*, 298–300.

p. 13, "In lending . . .": Anastaplo, *The Constitutionalist: Notes on the First Amendment*, 296–297.

p. 17, "After reading . . .": *Schenck v. United States*, 249 U.S. 47 (1919). Transcript of Record, file date: May 3, 1918, 42–48.

p. 17, "In a criminal . . .": *Schenck v. United States*, 60.

p. 18, "Under the First . . .": *Schenck v. United States*, 70.

pp. 18–19, "Thompson reminded . . .": *Schenck v. United States*, 66.

p. 19, "The records . . .": *Federal Reporter*, vol. 253, December 1918–January 1919. St. Paul, MN: West Publishing Company, 1919, 212–213.

pp. 20–21, "In a message to Congress . . .": Woodrow Wilson, "President Wilson's Declaration of Neutrality," Message to Congress, 63rd Cong., 2d Sess., S. Doc. 566, Washington DC, August 18, 1914, 3–4.

p. 21, "Campaigning under the . . .": Woodrow Wilson, "Speech before Joint Session of Congress," 65th Cong., 1st sess., 1917, S. Doc. 5, April 2, 1917.

p. 25, "It would be . . .": "New Police Arms Awe Socialists," *New York Times,* June 1, 1917, 1.

p. 26, "Created a week . . .": Robert A. Wells, "Mobilizing Public Support for War: An Analysis of American Propaganda During World War I," Annual Meeting of the International Studies Association, New Orleans, LA, March 24–27, 2002, http://isanet.ccit.arizona.edu/noarchive/robertwells.html

CHAPTER TWO

p. 30, "President Woodrow . . .": Woodrow Wilson to Edwin Y. Webb, May 22, 1917. Cited in "Wilson, Burleson, and Censorship in the First World War," by Donald Johnson, *Journal of Southern History*, 28:1, February 1962, 46–58.

pp. 30–31, "He said the . . .": Regin Schmidt, *Red Scare: FBI and the Origins of Anticommunism in the United States, 1919–1943*, Copenhagen, Denmark: Museum Tusculanum Press, 2000, 141–142.

p. 31, "A small group . . .": "Espionage Bill Called Despotic," *New York Times*, February 20, 1917, 2.

p. 31, "I would put . . .": "Senators Riddle Espionage Bill," *New York Times*, April 19, 1917, 1.

p. 32, "Under the bill . . .": "Opposes Spy Bill Section," *New York Times*, February 21, 1917.

p. 32, "Another section . . .": "The Espionage Bill," *New York Times*, April 13, 1917, 3.

p. 33, "If there should . . .": "Espionage Bill Hotly Attacked," *New York Times*, April 13, 1917, 3.

p. 33, "I am constantly . . .": "Espionage Bill Hotly Attacked."

p. 34, "Former newspaper . . .": "Senators See Peril in Espionage Bill," *New York Times*, April 15, 1917, 3.

p. 35, "The freedom . . .": "The Espionage Bill."

p. 35, "Were it possible . . .": "Press Fights Back to Hold Freedom," *New York Times*, April 20, 1917, 4.

p. 36, "One senator . . .": "Closure Proposed for Espionage Bill," *New York Times*, May 10, 1917, 9.

p. 37, "President Wilson continued . . .": "Wilson Demands Press Censorship," *New York Times*, May 23, 1917, 1.

p. 37, "He met with the . . .": "President Calls Conferees, Urges Press Censorship," *New York Times*, May 24, 1917, 1.

p. 37, "Representative George S. Graham . . .": "House Defeats Censorship Law by 184 to 144," *New York Times*, June 1, 1917, 1.

p. 38, "After the president . . .": "Espionage Bill Is Signed," *New York Times*, June 16, 1917, http://query.nytimes.com/mem/archive-free/pdf?res=9500EEDA123BE03ABC4E52DFB066838C609EDE

p. 39, "Beginning in the summer . . .": Brenda Roth, "Albert Sidney Burleson," *The United States in the First World War: An Encyclopedia*, London: Routledge, 1999, 114–115.

pp. 39, 42, "When the magazine's . . .": "Socialists to Test the Espionage Act," *New York Times*, July 10, 1917, http://query.nytimes.com/mem/archive-free/pdf?res=9804E5DB133BE03ABC4852DFB166838C609EDE

p. 40, "U.S. Attorney . . .": Francis Caffey, July 12, 1917, National Archives; cited in "The Emma Goldman Papers," *Berkeley Digital Library*, http://sunsite.berkeley.edu/Goldman/Guide/introduction.html

CHAPTER THREE

pp. 45–46, "Attorney General Thomas . . .": Walter Nelles, ed., *Espionage Act Cases*, New York: National Civil Liberties Bureau, 1918, 2.

p. 47, "In upholding . . .": "Brief for Charles T. Schenck," *Schenck v. United States*, 249 U.S. 47 (1919). Transcript of Record, file date: May 3, 1918, *The Making of Modern Law: U.S. Supreme Court Records and Briefs, 1832–1978*, Farmington Hills, MI: Gale Digital Collections, 2011, 6.

p. 48, "In Montana, . . .": "Montana Council of Defense Records: 1916–1921." Montana Historical Society Archives, http://nwda-db.orbiscascade.org/findaid/ark:/80444/xv22234

p. 48, "District Attorney Burton . . .": Curt Heimbuck, "R. L. Wyman and the Council of Defense," MonDak Heritage Center, February 1, 2006, www.mondakheritagecenter.org/history/wyman.html

p. 49, "Every German or Austrian . . .": Heimbuck, "R. L. Wyman and the Council of Defense."

p. 51, "Across the country, . . .": Clemens P. Work, director, The Montana Sedition Project, University of Montana School of Journalism, www.seditionproject.net/5profiles.html

p. 52, "North Dakota officials . . .": Ward Churchill and Jim Vander Wall, *Agents of Repression: The FBI's Secret Wars Against the Black Panther Party*, Cambridge: South End Press, 2002, 20.

p. 53, "I must be . . .": Eugene V. Debs, "Debs' Canton Speech," June 16, 1918. Chicago: Socialist Party of the United States, www.marxists.org/archive/debs/works/1918/canton.htm

p. 54, "These very gentry, . . .": Debs, "Debs' Canton Speech."

p. 54, "We Socialists . . .": Debs, "Debs' Canton Speech."

p. 57, "I would not . . .": "E. V. Debs Declines to Offer Defense," *New York Times*, September 12, 1918, http://query.nytimes.com/mem/archive-free/pdf?res=9400EED81439E13ABC4A52DFBF668383609EDE

p. 57, "The act . . .": "Find Debs Guilty of Disloyal Acts," *New York Times*, September 13, 1918, 1.

p. 58, "The jury found . . .": "Debs Arrested: Sedition Charged," *New York Times*, July 1, 1918, 1.

CHAPTER FOUR

p. 62, "How can a . . .": "Brief for Charles T. Schenck," *Schenck v. United States*, 249 U.S. 47 (1919). Transcript of Record, file date: May 3, 1918, 6.

p. 63, "You don't have . . .": "Brief for Charles T. Schenck," 7.

p. 63, "The lawyers questioned . . .": "Brief for Charles T. Schenck," 8–10.

pp. 63–64, "A review . . . ": "Brief for Charles T. Schenck," 14.

p. 64, "A conscript is . . .": "Brief for Charles T. Schenck," 14–15.

p. 64, "The prosecution . . .": "Brief for Charles T. Schenck," 18–22.

p. 65, "One person . . .": "Brief for Charles T. Schenck," 25–26.

p. 66, "No government . . .": "Brief for Charles T. Schenck," 30–31.

p. 67, "It was not . . .": "United States brief," *Schenck v. United States*, 249 U.S. 47 (1919). Transcript of Record, file date: May 3, 1918, *The Making of Modern Law: U.S. Supreme Court Records and Briefs, 1832–1978*, Farmington Hills, MI: Gale Digital Collections, 2011, 13.

p. 71, "A scene . . .": "Justice Holmes Succumbs to Pneumonia at Age of 93," *New York Times*, March 6, 1935, 1.

p. 72, "Scholars have praised . . .": Ronald K. L. Collins and David M. Skover, "Louis D. Brandeis Papers: *Ruthenberg v. Michigan*: An Introduction," *Supreme Court Review*, 2005, 333, www.law.harvard.edu/library/special/exhibits/digital/brandeis-papers.html

p. 72, "What I want . . .": R. L. Duffus, "Brandeis, 82 Today, Rounds Out a Philosophy," *New York Times*, November 13, 1938.

CHAPTER FIVE

p. 80, "Merely fighting . . .": *The Trial of Scott Nearing and the American Socialist Society (1919)*, New York: Rand School of Social Science, 1919, 256, www.scribd.com/doc/48240246/The-Trial-of-Scott-Nearing

p. 84, "Addressed to workers . . .": *Abrams v. United States*, 250 U.S. 616 (1919).

p. 84, "Officials charged . . .": *Abrams v. United States*, 250 U.S. 616 (1919).

pp. 90–91, "In a blistering . . .": A. Mitchell Palmer, "The Case Against the 'Reds,'" *Forum*, February 1920, 63:173–185, http://chnm.gmu.edu/courses/hist409/palmer.html

p. 92, "They were denied . . .": "Five Socialists Unseated by New York Assembly and Ousted from Chamber as Unloyal Citizens," *Morning Herald*, January 8, 1920, 1.

p. 93, "In December 1920 . . .": Richard Polenberg, *Fighting Faiths*, Ithaca, NY: Cornell University Press, 1987, 366–367.

p. 95, "The law made . . .": "Chap. 371," *Laws of the State of New York*, vol. 2. Albany, NY: J. B. Lyon, 1902, 958–960.

p. 95, "The magistrate . . .": Thomas C. Mackey, "'They are Positively Dangerous Men': The Lost Court Documents of Benjamin Gitlow and James Larkin Before the New York City Magistrates' Court, 1919," *New York University Law Review*, 69:421, 432–434.

pp. 95–96, "Does that say . . .": Clarence Darrow, "Darrow's Address to the Jury," *The Red Ruby*, New York: Communist Labor Party, 1920, 9.

p. 96 "Darrow observed . . .": Darrow, "Darrow's Address to the Jury," 12.

p. 96, "He would make America . . .": "The Gitlow Case (1920)," Clarence Darrow Digital Collection, University of Minnesota Law Library, http://darrow.law.umn.edu/trials.php?tid=14

CHAPTER SIX

p. 107, "During oral arguments . . .": Jay Walz, "Decision Is 6 to 2," *New York Times*, June 5, 1951, 1.

p. 110, "In one scene . . .": *Brandenburg v. Ohio*, 395 U.S. 444 (1969).

pp. 110–111, "The law, enacted . . .": Ohio Rev. Code Ann. 2923.13.

pp. 112–113, "The brief opinion, . . .": "ACLU 100 Greatest Hits," American Civil Liberties Union, www.aclu.org/Files PDFs/aclu_100greatest_hits.pdf

p. 117, "Today, *Brandenburg* . . .": Richard Miniter, "Is Terror Winning in the Courts?" American Civil Rights Union, 17, www.theacru.org/Is%20Terror%20Winning%20In%20 The%20Courts.pdf

p. 117, "The *Brandenburg* . . .": Robert H. Bork, letter to editor, *Commentary*, June 2005, 16. Cited in Miniter, "Is Terror Winning in the Courts?," 13–14.

p. 119, "The dangers . . .": Chris Montgomery, "Can *Brandenburg v. Ohio* Survive the Internet and the Age of Terrorism?: The Secret Weakening of a Venerable Doctrine," *Ohio State Law Journal*, 70:141, 163–166.

p. 119, "Governments are always . . .": Liz Garbus, director, *Shouting Fire: Stories from the Edge of Free Speech*. HBO Documentary Films, 2009.

p. 119, "The standard . . .": Ronald K. L. Collins, "Wartime Riskiest for Free Speech, Scholar Says," First Amendment Center, November 5, 2004, www.firstamendmentcenter.com/ analysis.aspx?id=14124

p. 120, "U.S. Attorney General . . .": Michael Kirkland, "WikiLeaks and the Espionage Act," United Press International, December 12, 2010.

p. 120, "In any event, . . .": Jim Sciutto and Lee Ferran, "Assange Lawyers Prepare for U.S. Spying Indictment," ABC News, December 10, 2010.

p. 121, "When dissenters . . .": Collins, "Wartime Riskiest for Free Speech, Scholar Says."

pp. 121–122, "As Justice Douglas . . .": William O. Douglas dissent, *Dennis v. United States*, 341 U.S. 494 (1951).

p. 122, "After two centuries . . .": Collins, "Wartime Riskiest for Free Speech, Scholar Says."

p. 122, "First Amendment scholar . . .": Collins, "Freedom's Risks: The Danger of Safety," First Amendment Center, April 2, 1010, www.firstamendmentcenter.com/commentary.aspx?id=22789

FURTHER INFORMATION

BOOKS

Chambliss, William J. *Courts, Law, and Justice*. Thousand Oaks, CA: Sage Publications Inc., 2011.

Collins, Ronald K. L., and Sam Chaltain. *We Must Not Be Afraid to Be Free*. New York: Oxford University Press, 2011.

Engdahl, Sylvia. *Free Speech*. San Diego: Greenhaven, 2007.

Fleming, Thomas. *Socialism* (Political Systems of the World). New York: Benchmark Books, 2007.

Marsico, Katie. *Woodrow Wilson* (Presidents & Their Times). New York: Benchmark Books, 2010.

Steffens, Bradley. *Free Speech*. Yankton, SD: Erickson Press, 2007.

WEBSITES

American Civil Liberties Union
www.aclu.org

Famous Trials
http://law2.umkc.edu/faculty/projects/ftrials/ftrials.htm

FindLaw (U.S. Supreme Court Cases)
www.findlaw.com/casecode/supreme.html

First Amendment Center
www.firstamendmentcenter.org

Law Library, American Law and Legal Information
http://law.jrank.org

Legal Information Institute, Cornell University Law School
www.law.cornell.edu

Oyez Project, U.S. Supreme Court Multimedia website
www.oyez.org

Supreme Court Historical Society
www.supremecourthistory.org

Supreme Court of the United States
www.supremecourt.gov

BIBLIOGRAPHY

ARTICLES

"ACLU 100 Greatest Hits." American Civil Liberties Union, www.aclu.org/FilesPDFs/aclu_100greatest_hits.pdf

"Allies Seek Plunder, Debs Tells Socialists," *New York Times*, June 17, 1918.

"Annuls Reds' Writ, but Grants Respite," *New York Times*, December 9, 1919.

Beiter, Greg. "100 Years of the American Socialist Party," *Justice*, no. 25, July–August 2001, www.oocities.org/cwibelfast/History/US-SPhistory.htm

Bork, Robert H. Letter to editor, *Commentary*, June 2005, 16.

"Brandeis Named for Highest Court," *New York Times*, January 29, 1916, 1.

Burnett, Paul. "The Red Scare," *Famous American Trials*, http://law2.umkc.edu/faculty/projects/ftrials/saccov/redscare.html

"A Byte Out of History: The Palmer Raids." Federal Bureau of Investigation. www.fbi.gov/news/stories/2007/december/palmer_122807

Chafee, Zechariah Jr. "Freedom of Speech in Time of War," *Harvard Law Review*, 32:932, 1919.

"Closure Proposed for Espionage Bill," *New York Times*, May 10, 1917, 9.

Cole, David. "Agon at Agora: Creative Misreadings in the First Amendment Tradition," *Yale Law Journal*, 95: 857–892 (1986).

Collins, Ronald K. L. "Freedom's Risks: The Danger of Safety." First Amendment Center, April 2, 1010, www.firstamendmentcenter.com/commentary.aspx?id=22789

Collins Ronald K. L., and David M. Skover. "What Is War?—Free Speech in Wartime," *Rutgers Law Journal*, 36: 3 (2005).

———. "Louis D. Brandeis Papers: Ruthenberg v. Michigan: An Introduction," *Supreme Court Review*, 333 (2005).

———. "Wartime Riskiest for Free Speech, Scholar Says." First Amendment Center, November 5, 2004, www.firstamendmentcenter.com/analysis.aspx?id=14124

"Convict 2 as Plotters: C.T. Schenk & Dr. Baer Ask New Trials in Philadelphia," *Washington Post*, December 21, 1917, 4.

"C. T. Schenk and Dr. Baer Ask New Trials in Philadelphia," *Washington Post*, December 21, 1917, 4.

Darrow, Clarence. "Darrow's Address to the Jury," *The Red Ruby*, New York: Communist Labor Party, 1920, 9.

Debs, Eugene V. "Debs' Canton Speech," June 16, 1918, pamphlet, Chicago: Socialist Party of the United States, 1918.

"Debs Arrested: Sedition Charged," *New York Times*, July 1, 1918, 1.

"Debs Is Released, Prisoners Joining Crowd in Ovation," *New York Times*, December 26, 1921, 1.

Duffus, R. L. "Brandeis, 82 Today, Rounds Out a Philosophy," *New York Times*, November 13, 1938.

"The Emma Goldman Papers," *Berkeley Digital Library*, http://sunsite.berkeley.edu/Goldman

"The Espionage Bill," *New York Times*, April 13, 1917, 3.

"Espionage Bill Called Despotic," *New York Times*, February 20, 1917.

"Espionage Bill Hotly Attacked," *New York Times*, April 13, 1917, 3.

"Espionage Bill Is Signed," *New York Times*, June 16, 1917.

"E. V. Debs Declines to Offer Defense," *New York Times*, September 12, 1918.

Fein, Bruce. "Squelching . . . the Inciters," *Washington Times*, August 9, 2005, A14.

"Find Debs Guilty of Disloyal Acts," *New York Times*, September 13, 1918, 1.

"Five Socialists Unseated by New York Assembly and Ousted from Chamber as Unloyal Citizens," *Morning Herald*, January 8, 1920, 1.

"General News Item," *Pennsylvania Medical Journal*, July 1919, 694.

Hamilton, Shane. "A Victor Without Peace." American History 102, University of Wisconsin, 1998, http://us.history.wisc.edu/hist102/bios/html/berger.html

Heimbuck, Curt. "R. L. Wyman and the Council of Defense." MonDak Heritage Center, February 1, 2006.

"High Court Adjourns for Van Devanter," *New York Times*, February 11, 1941.

"History Makers: Emma Goldberg." Jewish Women's Archive, http://jwa.org/historymakers/goldman

"History of the Socialist Party of Kansas." Sunflower Socialists, http://sunflowersocialists.org/history.html

"House Defeats Censorship Law by 184 to 144," *New York Times*, June 1, 1917, 1.

Hudson, David L. Jr. "Landmark Case Set Precedent on Advocating Force." First Amendment Center, June 8, 2009, www.firstamendmentcenter.org/analysis.aspx?id=21677

"J. C. M'Reynolds, the New Preceptor for the Trusts," *New York Times*, March 9, 1913.

Johnson, Donald. "Wilson, Burleson, and Censorship in the First World War," *Journal of Southern History*, 28:1, February 1962, 46–58.

"Justice Clarke Out of Supreme Court; to Work for League," *New York Times*, September 5, 1922, 1.

"Justice Day Resigns Supreme Court Seat," *New York Times*, October 25, 1922.

"Justice Holmes Succumbs to Pneumonia at Age of 93, *New York Times*, March 6, 1935, 1.

Kirkland, Michael. "WikiLeaks and the Espionage Act," United Press International, December 12, 2010.

Konkoly, Toni. "Famous Dissents: *Abrams v. United States* (1919)." Public Broadcasting Service, December 2006.

Linder, Doug. "Exploring Constitutional Law." University of Missouri-Kansas City Law School, 2011, http://law2.umkc.edu/faculty/projects/ftrials/conlaw/home.html

Mackey, Thomas C. "'They Are Positively Dangerous Men': The Lost Court Documents of Benjamin Gitlow and James Larkin Before the New York City Magistrates' Court, 1919," *New York University Law Review*, 69:421.

McBride, Alex. "The Supreme Court: Landmark Cases: *Schenck* v. *U.S.* (1919)." Thirteen/WNET New York, Educational Broadcasting Corporation, December 2006, www.pbs.org/wnet/supremecourt/capitalism/landmark_schenck.html

Miniter, Richard. "Is Terror Winning in the Courts?" American Civil Rights Union, 17, www.theacru.org/Is%20Terror%20Winning%20In%20The%20Courts.pdf

Mintz, S. "The Espionage and Sabotage Act." Digital History, www.digitalhistory.uh.edu/database/article_display.cfm?HHID=527

Moglen, Eben. "Holmes' Legacy and the New Constitutional History: Review of Owen Fiss," *Harvard Law Review*, March 6, 1995.

"Montana Council of Defense Records: 1916–1921." Montana Historical Society Archives, http://nwda-db.orbiscascade.org/findaid/ark:/80444/xv22234

Montgomery, Christopher. "Can *Brandenburg v. Ohio* Survive the Internet and the Age of Terrorism?: The Secret Weakening of a Venerable Doctrine," *Ohio State Law Journal*, 70:141, 163–166.

"New Police Arms Awe Socialists," *New York Times*, June 1, 1917, 1.

Novick, Sheldon M. "Justice Holmes and the Art of Biography," *William and Mary Law Review*, 33:4, 1237.

———. "The Unrevised Holmes & Freedom of Expression," *Supreme Court Review* 303 (1991).

O'Malley, Michael. "Free Speech, World War One, and the Problem of Dissent." Exploring US History, George Mason University, http://chnm.gmu.edu/exploring/20thcentury/freespeech

"Opposes Spy Bill Section," *New York Times*, February 21, 1917.

Palmer, A. Mitchell. "The Case Against the 'Reds,'" *Forum*, February 1920, 63:173–185.

Peck, Robert. "Overview: The First Amendment & Advocacy of Violence." First Amendment Center, www.firstamendmentcenter.org/faclibrary/overview.aspx?id=11452

"Pitney, Like His Father, Vigorous in Jersey Justice," *New York Times*, February 25, 1912.

"President Calls Conferees, Urges Press Censorship," *New York Times*, May 24, 1917, 1.

"Press Fights Back to Hold Freedom," *New York Times*, April 20, 1917, 4.

Ranney, Joseph A. "World War I and the Assault on Free Speech in Wisconsin." Wisconsin Legal History, www.wicourts.gov/courts/history/article37.htm

Roth, Brenda. "Albert Sidney Burleson," *The United States in the First World War: An Encyclopedia*. London: Routledge, 1999, 114–115.

Sciutto, Jim, and Lee Ferran. "Assange Lawyers Prepare for U.S. Spying Indictment," ABC News, December 10, 2010.

"Senators Riddle Espionage Bill," *New York Times*, April 19, 1917, 1.

"Senators See Peril in Espionage Bill," *New York Times*, April 15, 1917, 3.

"Socialist Leader & 3 Aids Taken," *Washington Post*, August 29, 1917, 3.

"Socialists to Test the Espionage Act," *New York Times*, July 10, 1917.

"Stone Is Nominated for Supreme Bench as M'Kenna Resigns, *New York Times*, January 6, 1925, 1–2.

Strassfeld, Robert N. "Espionage Act (1917) and Sedition Act (1918)." *Major Acts of Congress*, Encyclopedia.com, 2004.

"Supreme Court Rules Against Pacifists," *New York Times*, March 4, 1919, 10.

The Trial of Scott Nearing and the American Socialist Society (1919). New York: Rand School of Social Science, 1919.

"Tribute to Dead Jurist," *New York Times*, July 11, 1923.

"Van Devanter Hints He Might Quit Bench," *New York Times*, April 18, 1936.

Walz, Jay. "Decision Is 6 to 2," *New York Times*, June 5, 1951, 1.

"Was Young Lawyer in Lawless Land," *New York Times*, May 19, 1937.

Wells, Robert A. "Mobilizing Public Support for War: An Analysis of American Propaganda During World War I." Annual Meeting of the International Studies Association, New Orleans, LA, March 24–27, 2002.

Wilson, Woodrow. "President Wilson's Declaration of Neutrality." Message to Congress, 63rd Cong., 2d Sess., Senate Doc. No. 566, Washington DC, August 18, 1914.

———. "Speech before Joint Session of Congress," 65th Cong., 1st Sess., Senate Doc. No. 5, Washington DC, April 2, 1917.

"Wilson Demands Press Censorship," *New York Times*, May 23, 1917, 1.

"Wisconsin History." Kindred Trails, www.kindredtrails.com/Wisconsin_History-3.html

Wolgamott, L. Kent. "Emma Goldman: An Exceedingly Dangerous Woman," *Journal Star*, April 10, 2004.

Work, Clemens P., dir. "Montana Sedition Project." University of Montana School of Journalism, www.seditionproject.net

AUDIO/VIDEO

Bucklin, Mel. "Emma Goldman: An Exceedingly Dangerous Woman." *American Experience*. PBS/Nebraska Educational Telecommunications, documentary, 2004.

Garbus, Liz, dir. *Shouting Fire: Stories from the Edge of Free Speech*. HBO Documentary Films, 2009.

BOOKS

Anastaplo, George. *The Constitutionalist: Notes on the First Amendment*. Lanham, MD: Lexington Books, 2005.

———. *Reflections on Freedom of Speech and the First Amendment*. Lexington: University of Kentucky Press, 2007.

Bollinger, Lee. *The Tolerant Society*. New York: Oxford University Press, 1988.

Bollinger, Lee, and Geoffrey Stone, eds. *Eternally Vigilant: Free Speech in a Modern Era*. Chicago: University of Chicago Press, 2002.

Chafee, Zechariah Jr. *Free Speech in the United States*. Cambridge: Harvard University Press, 1941.

Churchill, Ward, and Jim Vander Wall. *Agents of Repression: The FBI's Secret Wars Against the Black Panther Party*. Cambridge: South End Press, 2002.

Emerson, Thomas. *The System of Freedom of Expression*. New York: Random House Trade Paperbacks, 1970.

Federal Reporter: Cases Argued and Determined in the Circuit Courts of Appeals and District Courts of the United States, vol. 253. St. Paul, MN: West Publishing Company, 1919.

Lewis, Anthony. *Make No Law: The Sullivan Case and the First Amendment*. New York: Random House, 1991.

The Making of Modern Law: U.S. Supreme Court Records and Briefs, 1832–1978. Farmington Hills, MI: Gale Digital Collections, 2011.

Nelles, Walter, ed. *Espionage Act Cases*. New York: National Civil Liberties Bureau, 1918.

Nesbit, Robert C. *Wisconsin, A History*. Madison: University of Wisconsin Press, 1973.

Parker, Richard A., ed. *Free Speech on Trial*. Tuscaloosa: University of Alabama Press, 2003.

Pohlman, H. L. *Justice Oliver Wendell Holmes: Free Speech & The Living Constitution*. New York: New York University Press, 1993.

Polenberg, Richard. *Fighting Faiths*. Ithaca: Cornell University Press, 1987.

Posner, Richard, *The Essential Holmes*. Chicago: University of Chicago Press, 1992.

Rabban, David, *Free Speech in its Forgotten Years*. New York: Cambridge University Press, 1999.

Stone, Geoffrey R. *Perilous Times: Free Speech in Wartime*. New York: W. W. Norton: 2004.

Tribe, Laurence, *American Constitutional Law*, 2nd ed. Eagan, MN: West, 1988.

Work, Clemens P. *Darkest Before Dawn: Sedition and Free Speech in the American West*. Albuquerque: University of New Mexico Press, 2006.

Zinn, Howard. *A People's History of the United States: 1492–present*. New York: HarperCollins, 2003.

COURT CASES/DOCUMENTS

Abrams v. United States, 250 U.S. 616 (1919).

Barron v. Baltimore, 32 U.S. 243 (1833).

Brandenburg v. Ohio, 395 U.S. 444 (1969).

Bridges v. California, 314 U. S. 252 (1941).

Debs v. United States, 249 U.S. 211 (1919).

Dennis v. United States, 341 U.S. 494 (1951).

Frohwerk v. United States, 249 U.S. 204 (1919).

Gitlow v. New York, 268 U.S. 652 (1925).

Laws of the State of New York, vol. 2. Albany, NY: J. B. Lyon, 1902.

Moynihan, Daniel Patrick. "Appendix A: The Experience of the First World War." *Report of the Commission on Protecting and Reducing Government Secrecy*, Washington, DC: U.S. Government Printing Office, 1997.

Noto v. United States, 367 U.S. 290 (1961).

Ruthenberg v. Michigan, 273 US 782 (1927).

Schenck v. United States, 249 U.S. 47 (1919).

Truax v. Corrigan, 257 U.S. 312 (1921).

United States v. Groeschl, Dist. of Kentucky (1917).

United States v. Hall, 248 Fed. 150, Dist. of Montana (1918).

United States v. Olivereau, W.D. Wash. (1918).

United States v. Ramp, D. Or. (1918).

United States v. Zimmerman, Dist. of Indiana (1918)

Whitney v. California, 274 U.S. 357 (1927).

Yates v. United States, 354 U.S. 298 (1957).

WEBSITES

American Civil Liberties Union
www.aclu.org

Clarence Darrow Digital Collection
http://darrow.law.umn.edu/trials.php?tid=14

Debs Collection, Cunningham Memorial Library
http://library.indstate.edu/about/units/rbsc/debs/debs-idx.html

Famous Trials
http://law2.umkc.edu/faculty/projects/ftrials/ftrials.htm

FindLaw (U.S. Supreme Court Cases)
www.findlaw.com/casecode/supreme.html

First Amendment Center
www.firstamendmentcenter.org

Law Library, American Law and Legal Information
http://law.jrank.org

Legal Information Institute, Cornell University Law School
www.law.cornell.edu

Oyez Project, U.S. Supreme Court Multimedia website
www.oyez.org

Supreme Court Historical Society
www.supremecourthistory.org

INDEX

Page numbers in **boldface** are photographs.

ABOUT THE AUTHOR

Susan Dudley Gold has worked as a reporter for a daily newspaper, managing editor of two statewide business magazines, and freelance editor and writer for several regional publications. She has written more than four dozen books for middle-school and high-school students on a variety of topics.

Her work, which includes series on American history and law, has won numerous awards, including Carter G. Woodson Honor Book, Notable Social Studies Trade Book for Young People, and several first-place awards in the National Federation of Press Women's communications contest. Her most recent books include several titles in the Landmark Legislation series, including *Americans with Disabilities Act* and *Freedom of Information Act*, and the four other books in this series. Gold is the author of a number of books on Maine history.

She and her husband, John Gold, own and operate a web design and publishing business in Maine. They have one son, Samuel; a granddaughter, Callie; and a grandson, Alexander.